SAWDUST
AND
INCENSE

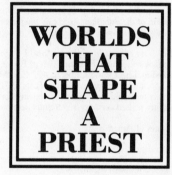

WORLDS
THAT
SHAPE
A
PRIEST

Gale D. Webbe

Foreword by Gail Godwin

ST. HILDA'S PRESS

Published by
ST. HILDA'S PRESS
% The Episcopal Diocese of Western North Carolina
P.O. Box 368
Black Mountain, North Carolina 28711

Distributed by
LONGSTREET PRESS, INC.
2150 Newmarket Parkway
Suite 102
Marietta, Georgia 30067

Printed in the United States of America

1st printing, 1989

Library of Congress Catalog Number 89-061687

ISBN 0-929264-65-7

This book was printed by R. R. Donnelley and Sons in Harrisonburg, Virginia.
The text type was set in Goudy Old Style by Typo-Repro Service, Inc., Atlanta, Georgia. Design and cover illustration by Paulette Lambert.

FOR KITTY

who helped immeasurably

CONTENTS

FOREWORD

Most of us carry around in our heads a short list of books that made a difference to our lives, special books that reached us at the right moment and thus helped to bring into being some aspects of ourselves we would not like to be without.

One of the books on my short list is Father Gale Webbe's *The Night and Nothing*. (It is also the favorite spiritual bedside book of Lily Quick in my novel *A Southern Family*.)

My first copy of *The Night and Nothing* "reached" me in London, in 1964, when I was, as usual, using my lunch hour to roam the shelves of Hatchard's bookstore in Piccadilly. In those days I was a young woman in search of sustenances more urgent to me than a midday sandwich—though I usually managed to squeeze that in, as well. The upstairs of Hatchard's was then—before its extensive remodeling—the quiet sanctuary for books on psychology, religion, and philosophy, and it was up to this somber, brownish room that I eagerly climbed, noonday after noonday, on the scent of what I needed. I needed news of how others had traveled creditably through the shadows and labyrinths of their own tricky, protean psyches and emerged into some measure of radiance.

Some days, up in the brown room, there would be a glimmer of light; some days there would be bonanzas; other days there would be nothing but the brown light and the ongoing search.

One bonanza day was when C. G. Jung's *Memories, Dreams, Reflections* appeared on the shelf:

> The decisive question for man is: Is he related to something infinite or not? That is the telling question of his life. . . . If we understand and feel that here in this life we already have a link with the infinite, desires and attitudes change.

And a few weeks after this, a familiar and beloved name flashed at me from the spine of a new publication. Gale D. Webbe's *The Night and Nothing*. So he was writing under his own name now, the spiritual mentor of my childhood in Asheville, North Carolina. This *was* news. When he had been rector of St. Mary's Episcopal Church in the late 1940s and early 1950s, he had always used a pen name—keeping his secular and sacred activities decorously divided. But all his parishioners were in on the secret of who "Stephen Cole" was: the prolific Stephen Cole, who dashed off amusing short stories and essays for national magazines; and who later published *The Hell of It: A Devil's Guide to Tempting Americans* ("twelve lectures given to a group of trainee-Devils in Hell by a senior tempter fiendishly well-versed in the contemporary American scene"). Said its foreword:

> The reader may be curious as to how this manuscript came into my possession. The answer is quite simple: I have been through Hell many times during my life, and one day I simply picked up the thing in passing . . .
> —S. C.

So it was a bonanza day indeed when I discovered *The Night and Nothing* in Hatchard's, a book that Father Webbe had at last signed his own name to. I of course bought a copy of the handsome little volume, with its purple and black dust jacket, and read it straight through that night in my boarding house in Chelsea.

I have been reading *in* it ever since. That first English edition is, alas, gone, lent to someone who never returned it, but I own two American editions, the earliest of which has been seized upon in so many needy hours that it literally falls open to the chapter I need most, the chapter on "Acedia." But that is another story. I simply want to make the point that I, along with many others, have a permanent place on my shelves for this pungently and compassionately written guide through the discouraging and demanding places on the spirit's journey.

In the penultimate chapter of *The Night and Nothing* comes this startlingly simple insight into eternity:

> Moments that are merely ours are essentially of no moment, being as trivial as the owner. When they are

shared with God they move over into eternity and eternity into them. The present moment is supernaturalized. Hence we are, often quite consciously, in eternal life now.

How serendipitously this echoes Jung's perception concerning our relationship to the infinite. The two insights enhance each other. One might even say they were *in dialogue* with each other: a phenomenon that we often find occurring among our indispensable books.

Father Webbe's second book published under his own name, *The Shape of Growth* (1985), has the cool, crisp, reflective aura of an autumn day. Drawing on the searchings of a long life, he compiles for us a guide to the stages of spiritual growth via the time-honored way of the great Christian mystics. *The Shape of Growth* is an austere book, more difficult than *The Night and Nothing*, but the older I get the better I like it. "Okay, you've come this far," the writer seems to be saying; "now, come a little farther." *The Shape of Growth* is not a book for sissies or dilettantes. Its opening sentence warns: "A perennial difficulty about 'self-expression' is that it requires and assumes something of a self to be expressed."

Sawdust and Incense: Worlds that Shape a Priest is a memoir, but it is a memoir of a special kind. It belongs to that literary genre called an *anatomy*: a narrative prose work in which bits and pieces and gleanings are assembled around a particular idea. The best-known example of this genre is probably *The Anatomy of Melancholy* (1621), by Robert Burton, who kept revising his vast and witty compendium on the highs and lows of the human psyche right up until his death in 1640. Burton, also, was an Anglican clergyman.

In *Sawdust and Incense*, a man who has lived attentively through all but the first of this American century's turbulent decades, and who has been a priest for more than five of those decades, discourses, in a variety of styles, upon the delicate and precarious art of letting the temporal world impinge upon us (and we on it) without losing touch with the eternal one. Our world, our many *worlds*, shape us, but the whole aim of a dedicated life is to refer our experience to its proper end: to give "the eternal now" its chance to break through, and transfigure, the mere present moment.

Father Webbe circles his subject from dozens of angles, ranging from reminiscence to satire. He gives us the flavor of what it was like to be the first married student at the General Theological Seminary in New York, sharing a Greenwich Village apartment house with a small monastic community because the seminary itself didn't have suitable accommodations for monks or married couples. He draws on his experiences as chaplain, and later headmaster, of a boys' school, and as husband, father, and parish priest. He tells us what it was like to be a clergyman who worked two summers as a paymaster on the Manhattan Project at Oak Ridge during World War II. (Talk about different worlds!)

There are chapters on everything from the special talents and occupational travails of clergy wives ("Isn't it too bad you're not a lady," murmurs an exacting old dowager as the rector's wife pours her tea), to the proper way to mount a horse, shoot in an archery tournament—or how to carve yourself a good hunting bow. The "sawdust" of the book's title, in fact, comes out of the writer's meditations on bow carving: the sawdust in this case being what is left over of us after the Master Bowyer, "discerning the bow latent within a billet of yew, carefully cuts away all excess and liberates the captive at the heart." Our "sawdust," in his extended metaphor, is made up of all our temporal leavings as we cooperate with our Maker in honing ourselves into our essential shape.

And, in a later chapter on creativity, he goes on to explain how our sawdust *is* our incense.

In this debonair and discursive memoir, playful chapters alternate with serious ones. Or a single chapter may begin in the guise of a simple adventure story (such as the time the rector goes to the hills to pan gold with a parishioner) and end up being a parable illustrating some aspect of the inner life. There are amusing "overviews" on the advance (or decline) of toys, automobiles, medicine, and other temporal necessities over the span of this American century. There is also a chilling account of a personal confrontation with solid evil; and there are the author's modest testimonies to some brushes with the uncanny as well as some inspired bouts of creativity.

Nestled throughout the whole memoir, like piquantly painted Easter eggs, are fascinating bits of lore about rectories ("Their architecture was curious. They were made of glass.") and about the people who inhabit them, the men and women whose chosen job requires them to be "set apart, yet constantly in touch." That's asking a lot, of course. It's asking that they live in two worlds and two time zones at once: the temporal—with all *its* interlocking and conflicting little worlds—and the eternal.

But that's what *Sawdust and Incense* is all about.

Gail Godwin
Woodstock, New York
March 1989

I seem to have been only like a boy playing on the seashore, and diverting myself in now and then finding a smoother pebble or a prettier shell than ordinary, whilst the great ocean of truth lay all undiscovered before me.

—Sir Isaac Newton

BEGINNINGS

ONE

Seminary

. . . he was not hatched from a special egg.

The hoary quip has it that we clergy are no better than we are because there's nobody but laymen (and women, nowadays) to make us from. In a measure that is true. The history of the average young cleric of either sex (for grammatical ease in capsuling it we can stay with the masculine gender) began about a quarter of a century ago with his being born in quite the normal manner—not hatched from a special egg. He then grew up as other boys do, unincubated in cotton wool and not noticeably odd throughout his grammar- and high-school years. In due time he went on to college, and even if it were not an agricultural school the possibilities are that he had opportunity to examine a stand or two of wild oats before graduation.

There being no such thing as a "pre-theological" course of study, our nascent clergyman simply went to the college of the general

3

ethos his parents considered wise for him and of his own particular selection from their suggested list. While there, if he seriously suspected in advance that he would go on to study for Holy Orders, he probably bore down most heavily on the humanities, ending up with an A.B. degree. Plenty of B.S. men (no pun intended) wind up in seminary, however.

For it is by no means probable, let alone certain, that he was planning on the priesthood when he went to college. The ways of God with man are mysterious and most personal, but the general truth is that somewhere along the line there can arise the notion that one might become a clergyman. The chosen one probably utters an astonished, perhaps even horrified, "Who, me?," briefly circles the dread idea, and then puts it aside or at least on a back burner.

The chances are that it is put aside often, as it continues to pop up again and again. Most understandably, and with good reasons, we do tend to resist the pull of this vocation, or at least to ponder it more searchingly than other possibilities for life's work. As a matter of fact, spiritual directors advise against entering the ministry unless one finds that he is firmly prevented from doing anything else. The heart of the matter is that we are dealing here with the Hound of Heaven, and He with us. Over the searching years, if the "call" is a genuine one, under His subtle leading the notion will grow to a feeling and the feeling to a certainty, or as near to certainty as one can get in a world where we see through a glass darkly. One then enters a seminary.

Now let's leave the general for the particular. My own "feeling," put aside from time to time during fifteen years, only became "certainty" as I was reading a story in the *Saturday Evening Post* two years after graduation from Amherst College. (Incidentally, I had chosen Amherst over Trinity for the significant reason that the former went in for intercollegiate swimming—my sport—and the latter did not. For lagniappe, Amherst was close to Mt. Holyoke and Smith. In the classic manner I dated Smith and married Mt.

Holyoke. Somebody else had brought her to the Beta dance, but I took her away.) I haven't the faintest idea, now, what that *Saturday Post* story was about. It simply "happened" along at the right time, after I had been plowed up by the Great Depression and was probing to find out who I really was and what I should really do, as will be outlined in due course.

Something having clicked at long last, and my wife being more than acquiescent, I set about fulfilling the requirements for getting into seminary. Our family doctor certified me as adequately sane and terribly healthy. The rector of our parish, who knew me quite well, and its vestry, some of whom had heard tell of me, approved me, possibly with some misgivings. The bishop of our diocese, a kindly man, looked with favor upon my application, and the seminary dean, a fearsome one, accepted me. So one day in late September, back when the Ninth Avenue elevated train was still clacking along, I stood outside the gates of the General Theological Seminary in New York City, gazing at "The General," as the stone statue of Moses over its main entrance is piously called by all students. Moses glared stonily back at me as I stood there in one final dither, wondering what it would be like inside.

I wondered about my classmates. Would they be scrawny, emaciated asthmatics with low blood pressure and poor coordination? If so, what would I do in the afternoons when they were all sitting in the chaplain's apartment on the edge of their chairs, tiny napkins on knees, drinking tea and making polite conversation? Would I have to go to the World Series alone? How would I keep in good physical shape, lacking any competition?

To get ahead a bit—it is probable that the basketball team of a certain university in New York shared these misconceptions. They came over to play the seminary team and at the start were kind, polite, considerate, deferential, and non-blasphemous. Clearly they did not want to harm either our bodies or our ideals. At the end they were probably a disillusioned group of young men, and certainly a badly beaten one. The seminary's team was a collection of former college stars and one of the best teams in the East. Had we had a football or boxing or track or swimming team, the story would have been the same.

Seminarians, in short, are college men and women a couple of years older, wiser, and better. You meet all kinds there, exactly as in college, except that you meet more kinds. I hadn't run across any monks at Amherst, which didn't go in for that sort of thing, but we had a few in seminary. Before three of these strange creatures became my closest friends, I watched them out of the corners of my eyes, among other things marveling at how they managed to cross intersections through New York's traffic clothed in their flowing monastic garb. (The answer to that is simple, by the way. New York's police department, Irish Catholic to the core, unable to distinguish between a "Protestant" monk and a "Catholic" one and preferring to be safe rather than eternally sorry, stopped traffic indiscriminately for both varieties. Modern traffic lights play no favorites.) For the first few days I was polite to our monastics and solemnly discussed African missions with them, while they stood patiently by with arms folded and hands piously inside opposite sleeves, as was their public rule. Later on, when they came over to visit us in our apartment, those same pious hands concealed in voluminous sleeves would emerge with a couple of long-stemmed roses or a coffee pot for my wife and a bottle of near-beer or a breviary for me. Throughout the three seminary years, we lived cheek by cowl.

The seminary didn't know what to do with me, its first married student (at least half of them are married these days), and didn't have accommodations for us, so we lived outside the close. Our monks had to live in secluded community and somewhat differently from other folk, so they too lived outside. For these opposite reasons—their celibacy and our married state—we wound up neighbors in Greenwich Village apartments owned by a chapel of Trinity Parish.

Incidentally, I earned our rent and utilities by running one of our chapel's Boys' Clubs. My wife earned our cash income—thirty dollars a month—by tending its four busy altars, by which I do mean

6

being the parish's entire Altar and Flower Guild. Our dollar a day sufficed to feed us and occasionally even let us take in *Hamlet* or *The Green Pastures* and hear Paul Whiteman's orchestra doing "Rhapsody in Blue." Museums were free, of course. Subway rides did cost nickels, but when necessary we scraped those up by turning in empty milk bottles scavenged from trash cans. My classmates had similar, and dissimilar, ways to make ends meet. Now that everybody's dead it can safely be disclosed that winnings from blue-haired ladies at uptown Bridge Clubs put Bob—we'll call him that— through seminary. His skill at the game was world-class. I'm afraid theirs wasn't.

That seminary class, surely a typical one, was made up of mature young men—I repeat that there were no women seminarians back then—of high individual dedication, comprising a group with collective purpose different from that of my college class. Our college class was close-knit and, nearly sixty years later, still is, but its individual members were all ultimately going in separate directions. My seminary classmates, at graduation, also went in separate directions, but in a common cause. That makes a difference.

Most of that long-ago group of fellow-students served with lifelong fidelity as honored and beloved rectors of parishes. A few followed special vocations: Jud became a medical doctor and a psychiatrist; Jonesey spent most of his ministry as an Army chaplain, serving all over the world. A couple of my classmates became bishops, and several others came to positions high in the councils of the Church.

Tommy, one of my monks, became a secular priest working with slum waifs and ultimately founded a Boys' Town with a select clientele—his boys had to come to him from jail. With an uncanny ability he straightened them out and got them started on the proper road. The home still flourishes, but Tommy died, years ago, of a heart attack.

Joe too is in The Church Expectant. I like to remember that on the eve of his ordination he had me lock him in the church to keep knightly vigil on his knees before the sacrament, and that it was I who turned him loose next morning into a world that needed his dedicated fire. Down the years I often rewarmed my own heart at his steady flame, mostly on visits to him in Utah and New Mexico. Joe spent his long earthly life in ministry to our American Indians—he was the only Caucasian I know who was adopted into the Paiute tribe. A sensitive and able poet, author of several books, recipient of an honorary Doctor of Letters degree, a fine athlete, Joe was most at home riding horseback down a canyon or living in a hogan. When on a visit back East he preached for me in Newark, New Jersey, the only picture of him I could find for publicity was of Joe astride a horse, the Buckaroo Priest. The *Newark Evening News* didn't care to run that sort of thing on its church page, so it cut the horse out from under him.

Curly, who came from Colorado, began his ministry there in a place so high in the mountains that it snows every month of the year. During long winters when the town is completely isolated, a certain restlessness begins to beset the citizens, and perhaps especially the students at a local junior college. When we lived in Kansas, we visited Curly there for a week of fishing the Gunnison River and learned from him that a fair amount of his pastoral counseling during the winters, back there before The Pill, began by his saying to errant young couples who sought his advice, "As a priest I can't tell you what to do, but I can say you'd better do it quickly. Now let's talk about it."

I have an especially soft spot in my heart for Dick because it was he whom God the Holy Ghost employed as His chief agent in getting me to North Carolina. As will be disclosed, Dick and I went from the seminary to western Kansas to work for a time in "domestic missions" before returning to our home diocese. Dick left Kansas before I did, in order to try his vocation as a monk, and while he was so doing, a Tarheel priest happened to visit the monastery, happened to mention that a church boarding school down his way needed a chaplain, and happened to ask Dick if he could suggest somebody for that work. Dick happened to think of me. Back then the Holy Ghost worked solely through people in the subtle and basic

8

matter of a particular call. In these last days He is learning how to use a computer.

Dick, to return to him, discovered during his novitiate, without the aid of a computer, that he was neither a contemplative nor a celibate. Ultimately he married a girl who had, curiously enough, tried her vocation as a nun and had come to similar personal conclusions. This fine lady still lives, but Dick died of a heart attack long ago, after years of inner-city work in Los Angeles. I had happened to be conducting a teaching mission for him in the Watts area when those riots erupted around us there a couple of decades ago.

There were some forty of us in that class, so I could go on and on. It must suffice to say that to have been a close friend and co-worker with all those men, living and dead, was and remains a vast privilege. The statue of Moses kept its stony silence about them because it couldn't tell me these things. You learn them by living and dying together.

You also learn the falsity of stereotype. Episcopalians are dubbed "God's frozen people" who scorn vitality and fear enthusiasm. The Episcopal Church is widely known as "the conservative party at prayer," that prayer of course being the prayer of the Pharisee. Sometimes, in kindness if not accuracy, we hear that our Church's vocation is to keep the brains of the country Christian. Above all it is asserted that even the saints which Anglicanism occasionally produces are sedate, that we have no heroic saints. Nonsense. History records hundreds of flaming Anglican heroes. Even I myself have personally known a few. For openers I give you Tommy and Dick and Joe.

Another query I had for "The General" was in the intellectual line. Like everybody else, I knew that many years ago a former professor at the General Seminary had written his famous little poem "A Visit From St. Nicholas." That was nice, of course, but I didn't believe in Santa Claus. I wondered about the acumen of kindly old theological professors with long gray beards. I wondered if they, and indeed the Church, had faced the challenges of science and evolution and psychology and all the "isms" of the restless new age in which I had grown up.

College, that marvelous experience, had opened the eyes of my mind, disclosing a wide horizon unrealized in childhood. It had left me in awe of the endless possibilities of life and knowledge; puzzled by the apparent contradictions in the scheme of things; overwhelmed by the multiplicity of tenable positions. College raised questions, validly risking the inevitable danger that one might be left rootless and groundless, groping in a labyrinth for the way out. Would my best policy in seminary be to throw questions, intellectual bombshells, all around the place, thus possibly wakening those sleepy old men who went around quoting the Bible? Still with some reservations, I finally opened the gates of the great quadrangle and went in.

Within forty-eight hours I learned that the sleepy old men on the faculty were wide-awake sharp-minded scholars of international recognition, who did not believe that Christianity was compatible with mediocrity in any field, including the intellectual. They knew all the questions that life and college had raised in me, plus some new and fancy ones. They also set about answering those questions. They put the end of a string into your hands so that you could indeed find your way out of that labyrinth—and thus, later on, be able to serve as a guide to others.

Seminary is a graduate school, of course, so quite properly it operates on a higher and more difficult level than that of college. Furthermore, a ruthless intellectual honesty pervades the place. The faculty shows no trace of closed or narrow mind, of willful blindness to undesired facts, of wishful thinking. Hence they hone your mind so that you will not too often indulge in sloppy thinking. They prepare you to meet intellectual difficulties on their own ground, and thus to help others do the same. But above and beyond that—or involved in that—is the main and higher point: seminary study and life brought to me and my classmates what the world desperately needs—order, purpose, an integrating principle in life and for life.

In great degree this awareness of cosmos rather than chaos seeped into us also because in seminary, probably for the first time—except in the case of those monks—we learned to pray systematically, in earnest and in depth. The faculty didn't *make* us pray; after all, that cannot be done. There were indeed daily services, frequent special devotional events like quiet days and retreats, and courses in ascetical and mystical theology. There was also a total atmosphere leading toward prayer, plus close association with some very holy people. But perhaps above all, in seminary we learned about evil, and thus began to see the necessity for prayer. More about that in a moment, after we back up for a fresh start.

They put us into parishes to learn some practical aspects of our coming trade under the guidance and supervision of an experienced priest, lest later memories of blunders in our own early ministry be too saddening. In that milieu and process we began to learn some of the inside truth about people as well as something of their outer pressures—like families of fourteen people being forced to "live" in one tenement room. Perhaps most important, in that work we began learning something far more basic than pastoral techniques. We began to glimpse the essence and heart of ministerial priesthood.

To state this in an exaggerated way: when I first began working with these underprivileged people it seemed to me that they left me no time I could call my own. They scheduled their surgery to suit their own conveniences, giving never a thought to mine. They contracted pneumonia whenever they pleased, indifferent to my important schedule. They suffered accidents at two A.M. and at that hour had the emergency room tell me about it, regardless of my need for rest. They attended Juvenile Court, as its central attraction, uncaring that I should be in a tutorial at the time. They even beat on my door when I was enjoying a most delicate and intimate colloquy with the Holy Ghost, not only interrupting Him but driving Him clean away.

11

Their casual assumptions irritated me at first. I thought they were taking it far too much for granted that I was entirely at their service. Then in a rare moment of grace one day I saw that that was precisely the point. I *was* at their service if in any real way I was to be their minister. The whole cherished concept, a legacy from Adam and Eve, that I was the center of the universe and that there were certain things that were "mine"—my smooth routine, my favorite chair, my time—completely inhibited any genuine ministry to others. Through these demanding, even at times exploitive, people, God was showing me what I would be getting into and also how I could get out of it.

I could get out of it by progressively getting out of myself, by dropping concern about *me* and turning my eyes, not to mention my mind and heart, outward toward *them*. If I could do so, by His help, there would be some hope that one day I might actually become an adequate minister. Ultimately, on this course I might even find not only usefulness in ministry, but also fulfillment and joy in priesthood—in living between two worlds reconciling man and God.

That is easier seen than really perceived; easier said than done. But, to glance ahead in time, God keeps at His loving work of chipping away at our defenses until they are all knocked down and at last we step out to stand free. He does this in strange little ways, using the material at hand. In silly example, early in my parish ministry I unduly valued "my" Monday off, so God saw to it that I was called upon to conduct three funerals that day, trusting that all those tears would wash away petty personal irritation and clear my sight.

Insight into ultimate levels of this truth about ministerial priesthood comes later, as a rule. In time we learn that the Holy Spirit, far from being driven away by some rude knocking at the door, in actual fact gladly accompanies us, indeed opens His heart to us and ours to Him, as we speed toward the hospital in the wee small hours.

Still later on we begin to learn in whatsoever state we are, therewith to be content. There to serve, in the here and now, the only time and place it can be done.

Lastly we learn that we are completely expendable, in every sense of the word, at any time, and that we volunteered for our duty in the front lines where the battle is fiercest but where we have been trusted to hold the fort until clearly relieved by the High Command.

In seminary my friend Brother John told us all this very clearly, but we did not really hear him then. Because we had asked him, but only because we had asked him about it, he was telling us of the privations and hardships in the African mission station where he had served with two other monks for several years, until his Order called him back to America for further theological education and ordination to the priesthood. He told a harrowing tale. The least of their difficulties was that their American bodies were not adapted to African climate, so he and the two others were more than half sick all the time. Every morning all of them would take their temperatures; the one with the lowest degree of fever made breakfast.

At the end of the account somebody asked Brother John if, after seminary, he was going back to Africa. John was amazed. "Why, of course," he said.

Now let's get back to that matter of evil. The seminary chaplain sent us out working in the slums, grubbing around in the cesspools of New York. Here we hobnobbed with thieves, racketeers, ward heelers, and what-not. (In those days, as I found out from personal offers, the going rate for voting the proper ticket in my ward was seventy-five cents or a pint of gin, take your choice.) On occasions we hobnobbed with murderers. My friend Curly spent one long evening in a murky dive trying to talk a hit-man out of committing a murder-for-hire that night. He failed, so when the man left to fulfill his contract, Curly had no recourse except to come back to the seminary chapel to pray for him and for his victim.

In college, humanism had been sufficient for most of us. We idealistic youths wanted, after graduation, to join with other well-intentioned folk in the challenging, but essentially simple, task of improving the human scene, in sure and certain hope of human perfectibility via natural means. The more blatantly cocksure ideal-ists among us were even more direct about this, confident that they could take the human race by the shoulders, shake it, and set it straight single-handedly and willy-nilly.

In seminary, where we began to feel the enormous dynamic of a desperately fallen world and to learn the misery of its hopeless prisoners, we discovered that humanism is not enough. So we began to bring God into the fray, and to lift the fray into God. Thus we learned that God is very real, that He knows a vast deal about His world and its people, and is willing and able to step in to help the sorry mess along.

Insight into a higher level of this truth came to me while Tommy, Dick, and I were making our preordination retreat at Holy Cross monastery, perched on its eminence high above the Hudson River. On the third afternoon of that retreat, as I was stretching my legs along a wooded path I came upon a statue of the Madonna with her Holy Child in her arms. I may have lingered for a moment before it, perhaps thankful that there still were people who set reminders of the supernatural here and there in the midst of this naughty world.

Strolling further down the path I turned a corner and came across a second statue of the Madonna and Child. This time the Child was represented as a youth perhaps seven or eight years old. He was standing at his mother's side. Her hand was on his shoulder. I paused, looked, thought nothing of any consequence, and passed by on the other side.

A little later the path turned a third corner, where I en-countered still a third statue. This time it was of the Virgin Mary alone. Her Child was gone. She stood there empty-handed, looking at me. In a manner of speaking, talking to me. "Take care of Him," she said, quoting from the parable of the Good Samaritan. "I took care of Him in His babyhood. I took care of Him in His boyhood and youth. Now He is gone from me. Now, *you* take care of Him."

I did not, on that occasion of a preordination retreat, dwell on the presumption in my thought; on the posturings and conceit of us who mess up a third-rate planet circling a fifth-rate star in a tenth-rate galaxy in a remote corner of the universe and nevertheless allege we can take care of God, or indeed that He needs care. Of course God cannot be hurt—He is impassible, as the theologians put it. I simply accepted, then as now, that once upon a time, out of all the planets in the universe, God came to dwell upon this abandoned one—doubtless because it needed it the most, but in any case He came here. It might have been simpler to blow it up, but that was not the course then taken. Therefore a manger in a stable in a village called Bethlehem and a cross on a hill outside Jerusalem set the seal upon this our outpost as being of some significance, possibly of unique significance, in the value-system of a Mind greater than ours. Furthermore, in coming here the impassible God as it were put His hand into the world, and that hand can be torn and bloodied. He did not merely put his impersonal values here. He put His very Person here, and as a matter of historical fact that Person was grievously abused and even temporarily destroyed. From the beginning He needed care, and has continued to need it ever since, down the savage centuries.

I repeat that I did not then dwell on thoughts of that kind. Nor did I spend time considering that the values of God—items like truth and beauty and righteousness—will surely abide and ultimately triumph because they are of His almighty Being. I simply thanked the Lady for her graciousness in caring enough for me to stop me in my path, and at her bidding took as my life's motto and ideal the one that all clergy do— "Take care of Him."

Our parishioners know, from great cause and with great clarity, how far short of that ideal we fall. It may be that they also discern a greater truth—that it is indeed our ideal.

After three too-short years of seminary we passed our canonical exams, were ordained, and immediately put our collars on backward. New York's finest then began stopping traffic for us. That didn't last long, however, for soon we all scattered to the four winds. All but Tommy and Dick and I who, far from scattering, headed out together for western Kansas, the center of the Dust Bowl in the middle of the Dust Bowl years.

TWO

Black Blizzard

. . . I passed by on the other side—a Biblical maneuver,
to be sure, but not an honored one.

I have suffered considerable ennui lately because of my friends'
gripes about the weather—my present and pampered friends in
North Carolina, that is, whom we will soon begin to meet in these
pages. Let the heat roll up into the low nineties, with equal humidity—or, on the other hand, let the thermometer drop into the
twenties so that skim ice begins to form—and they start to moan
long words like "unbearable" and "insufferable," while they endure
until some savior appears with a tray of frosted juleps or hot toddies,
whichever the situation calls for.

Well, maybe I complain too, and certainly I reach for the
enabling refreshment. But in the back of my mind there is the
memory of weather that was really weather. Kansas weather.

There is the memory of a long-ago summer in western Kansas,
before air conditioning, when the temperature reached 121 degrees

one warm afternoon, and stood at over a hundred degrees for fourteen days at a stretch, with the popcorn in the fields going crazy—and some of the citizens with it. There is the recollection of a scourge of Kansas locusts, which is a visitation guaranteed to get your mind off petty troubles. There was also a Kansas winter, with the thermometer way down yonder and a blizzard blowing straight off the North Pole—but you read about that sort of thing in the newspapers last year. I also recall vividly a Kansas twister, which performed its usual acts of God, including the demolition of the Presbyterian Church, so that thereafter the Methodists and Episcopalians remained in unrivaled possession of the field, beyond question to the greater glory of God. Best—or worst—of all, I have had personal experience of that most horrendous meteorological freak, the Kansas dust storm (and I don't mean the comparatively mild spring dusters that western Kansas occasionally has at the present time).

The Kansas dust storm I remember is not the kind of weather that griping and mint juleps can contend with. Rather, it is downright disastrous and dangerous, like those better-known menaces—the hurricane, the tornado, and the earthquake.

I encountered my first dust storm on a hot day in January—Kansas easily manages weather like that. With the temperature in the high seventies I was driving along the highway some miles west of Garden City when my eyes happened to rove toward the northern horizon. There I noticed a thing that moved me to mild curiosity—a black wall that stretched from skyline to skyline and moved rapidly higher and higher as I watched it.

From time to time I glanced idly at the strange phenomenon, and I even continued to idle when a couple of automobiles scuttled past me at about eighty miles an hour. But the driver of the third such car was waving his arm wildly as he swished by; he looked as if he were urgently trying to tell me something that would be good for my health. So I began to feel slightly uneasy, especially since the thing on my right had exploded until it filled the entire northern half of the sky. I immediately pressed my foot harder on the accelerator.

Then, suddenly, the approaching menace was only half a mile away, and I could see it clearly. It was a wall of dust towering high into the sky, its whole forward surface a writhing, twisting fury of air-tossed Russian thistle. My car windows were open, so I could hear the wind behind the storm roaring with the voice of a dozen freight trains. I slowed and began to roll up the windows. But I was still going at a fair rate of speed when the blast struck me, blowing my automobile completely across the road. Then the world blacked out. I was swallowed up in dust.

Automatically, in the tumultuous choking darkness, I switched on the headlights. For a moment I thought that the wiring had failed, until I realized that this dust was opaque—so completely dense that I could not even see my own lights. I stopped the blind and plunging car as quickly as possible and turned on the heater, for it was beginning to get cold. (Incidentally, the thermometer dropped forty degrees in thirty minutes, and that night reached a low of seventeen below.)

With the motor turning over slowly, I sat and considered my plight. Home was fifty miles back, but there was a crossroads village less than ten miles ahead. If I could go anywhere, it seemed best to drive there, for surely I could not fight this storm for any distance. Perhaps I had better stay where I was? But that might be as dangerous as driving because I was on the main highway, and no doubt there were other cars abroad which could at any moment run into me. The thought was not pleasant.

I had to spit to clear my mouth of dust, and then I began to think of my wife back home. Perhaps she was somewhat curious about how I was making out in this new brand of weather that doubtless had swept over her too. For that matter, where had she been when the storm struck our town? I wiped the dust from my face and found my forehead slightly sticky with the sweat of fear. No, I wouldn't sit still where I was. I must go ahead and find a telephone. The quicker the better.

19

Perhaps by leaving the car for a minute or two I could get my bearings on the road through feeling for the curbs. I could then drive a few yards and repeat the performance. How long would it take to drive ten miles that way? Yet it was all I could think of.

Leaving the motor running and the lights on, I got out on the leeward side. The screaming wind whipped my hat from my head, tore the door from my grip, and slapped menacingly at my clothes. I bent behind the shelter of my trembling car and covered my streaming eyes with my hand. The choking dust was absolutely black; I tried to see my fingers an inch from my eyes and could not.

Holding with one hand to the car door, I reached down with the other and found concrete pavement beneath me. I was still on the highway, then. But on what part of it? I remembered having been blown over to the left side of the highway just before the storm struck; had I come back? I could not recall. It was possible that I was straight in the path of any oncoming traffic.

It would be necessary to move away from my car to find out about that. Yet suppose another car was plowing along through the storm right now? It would surely run me down, for I would never be able to see it or hear it. I couldn't even hear my own motor running, three feet away, through the howling roar of the wind. If I stretched out on the concrete pavement, searching for the edge of the road, a truck could come along and crush me. I thought of snakes I had run over on the highway and finally shrugged my shoulders. The chance had to be taken.

Averting my face from the buffeting wind that hissed under my car, I lay flat on the road, with my feet touching the running board, and groped over the pavement with outstretched hand as far as I could but failed to reach the curb. So far, all was well—I was at least seven feet from the wrong side of the road. Now if I crawled straight away from the car and located the far edge of the highway, I would know my exact bearings.

It was one of the more foolish decisions I have arrived at in a foolish life. Why I wasn't satisfied with seven feet of pavement I don't know even now. The only excuse for my complete stupidity through this whole episode is that it was my first brush with a dust storm.

In any case, I shuffled forward on hands and knees, hunching my shoulders in a futile attempt to shield my face. I had long since closed my useless eyes. About fifteen feet from the car, as nearly as I could tell, I felt the opposite curb. Again I spat and panted my relief that my car was in the correct lane. Then I turned around carefully, faced the searing blast, and prepared to start back for the car, resolved to try some driving. The highway, like all Kansas roads, ran interminably straight on, doubtless in an endeavor to get to Colorado as quickly as possible. Perhaps I could drive for quite a distance before I had to perform this stunt again.

I shielded my smarting eyes against the driving dust and looked up to see if I could locate my car. Surely I should be able to make out the lights, viewing them as I was from the side. But the car had disappeared. There was not even a glimmer of light visible.

I must confess that I knew a brief moment of panic, of being hopelessly lost in a formless void, but that soon passed. After all, my foot was still in contact with the curb, and I could tell that I was heading in the correct direction. All I had to do was crawl straight forward and I would bump into the automobile. Thus I reassured myself and started crawling as straight as I could and with head down to shield my eyes as much as possible from the dust.

With great care I counted the number of times I moved my hands forward, trying to advance them about a foot at a time. When I had counted to twenty, and then to twenty-five, without encountering anything solid, I knew that I had missed the car.

I stopped. In what direction did safety lie—right or left? There was no way of knowing, and to make a wrong guess could be disastrous. I cursed the furious darkness, and then cursed myself for not having first tried the road on the windward side of the car.

This second panic having passed, I considered the possibility of continuing to crawl across the road until I found the curb on the side where my car stood. I could then walk, with one foot brushing the curb so that I would keep in a straight line and with my left arm outstretched. If my car lay within a few feet of the edge of the road, I would find it.

Of course, if it were out of reach, I would miss it entirely, and then all sense of location would be gone. Right now I was surely within five feet of safety. The other way, if I failed, I might be hopelessly lost. There was no such thing as a sense of direction in this absolute chaos.

The pavement was beginning to hurt my knees—I was still kneeling there, hunched over like a blizzard-driven steer—and I was sure I had worn through my trousers. So I told myself that I might as well be comfortable while I could and shifted carefully to sit down. As I settled into position, my shoulder struck painfully against something solid. My eager hands explored it. It was the rear bumper of my automobile. Believe me, I crawled into that old Pontiac as if it had been Noah's Ark.

From there on, my luck was in, because snow soon began to accompany the dust, and in a few minutes I was in the midst of a white blizzard instead of a black one. A windshield wiper will, for a while, take care of a normal blizzard, even in Kansas, so I quickly turned my car around and headed happily back for home.

This seems the proper time to tell you how my wife made out in that same storm, for her experience illustrates indoor life at such times. She knew of the storm's coming in advance because a friend telephoned when the official warning came through. My wife ran to the front window to watch the band of black, like a cloud bank, across the northern horizon—and to watch the frightened cars race down the highway, seeking sanctuary. She tells me that she began to wonder where I was and how I was faring.

In an incredibly short time, the storm was almost upon the town. Up on the little hill the school disappeared; then the mayor's house blotted out. Then, suddenly, the houses across the street vanished in a wall of black, and our bungalow shuddered and groaned as a tremendous wind hit it broadside. A second later, my wife was groping in the pitch black for a light switch.

22

When she found my desk lamp and turned it on, the air in the room was already foggy. There was a halo of dust around the light. Fine dust was streaming in around the window frame. She coughed and in a few minutes had to retire to the bathroom at the rear of the house, where the dust was less intense. There she ran water into the bathtub and soaked a sheet in it. Then, dragging a couple of chairs from the living room, she arranged the dripping sheet over them and sat beneath it on the floor. It was a whole lot easier to breathe under the wet cloth. So she sat and waited in a kind of cosmic loneliness.

When I contrast my blundering activity in that storm with my wife's patient and resourceful common sense in the same situation, I am moved to many humble thoughts. However, in short order we both became experts in dealing with the strange new adversary, for after that initiatory episode we experienced dozens of the storms—they continued until the thin vegetation of March and April gave Mother Earth something to cling to. And let me say here that I gained a high respect for human nature from that Kansas winter. People have hidden resources that enable them to adapt to anything—adapt in their physical way of living and, more importantly, in their spirit. The analogy may seem farfetched, but having seen the way that ordinary folk managed to come through a siege of dust storms makes me quite optimistic about them if they should ever have to face atomic bombardment. Human nature, in short, can be rather great when it has to be.

Some of our subsequent storms were mild—not more than a haze that hung suspended for one or several days until a light wind blew it away. The force of gravity was no help in clearing the air; gravity couldn't get hold of those tiny particles of dust, which seemed to be hundreds of times finer than talcum powder. I suppose they had been whirled and ground against each other until there wasn't anything left to whirl and grind away. Logically, that should bring us down to the atom, and I wouldn't be at all surprised if such were the truth of the matter. For short of an atom or its reasonable facsimile, what could filter into a hermetically sealed house—I'll tell you about this in a moment—and then take up lodgement inside a tight new refrigerator? But that dust did it, even in the course of a mild storm—one that centered somewhere else and was just a leftover in our area.

Others of those later storms were of the bang-up variety chronicled above, only of greater duration. Sometimes the wind blew the dust intermittently for a couple of days at a time. Against the fury of these things, we devised a system of taping up all the windows and doors in the house—even to the keyholes—with two-inch sealing paper, leaving only one door free as a means of exit and entrance. It helped a lot but left a lot more to be desired. We ate dust with every meal, breathed dust at every moment, smudged dust on every book and magazine, and wrote dusty letters to our friends. Dust was simply the omnipresent enemy, inside the house no less than outside it.

It began to get on our nerves, if I may indulge in an understatement. But we couldn't stay in our house bickering all the time, nor could the rest of the embattled town, and so every now and then somebody found himself in a hand-to-hand battle with Nature, Kansas style. One of the really rip-snorting black blizzards hit when a friend of mine was out in his back yard feeding his dogs, and he immediately became the only sober person I ever knew who got lost in broad daylight thirty feet from his own back porch.

He had a floodlight erected on the back of his house, which under normal circumstances turned night into day. His wife switched on that light when he became engulfed in the storm, and then she stood in the door screaming to him. She was a screamer of the thousand-decibel variety, too; but, for the most part, he neither saw nor heard a thing. Only once in a while, during a temporary lull, could he make out her faint whisper and glimpse a fitful spark where that floodlight should have been. Guided by those intervals, he finally made his way home, across his own croquet court, in thirty minutes.

To give you one last indication that those storms really cut out the light, let me recount the classic incident. Several of our towns-

24

folk were cooped up inside a lawyer's house, enduring one of the worst of our black blizzards, when the lawyer's son-in-law went to the front window and, hands in disconsolate pockets, stared out for a while. Finally he cried, with great relief in his voice, "By gosh, I think it's getting lighter out there!" But it turned out that his conclusion lacked real evidence, for he had been looking out a window that had been covered with tar paper and completely boarded up.

The bad storms produced the total blackness of a cave, but far worse than that was the loss of any sense of direction that you experienced when caught out in them. You were isolated in the roaring void that existed before creation, when the points of the compass had not yet been invented. Undoubtedly, that was the experience of those three farm children who were playing in the barn, a short distance from their house, when a storm descended upon them. They were found dead the next day, suffocated and frozen and scattered, but not one of them was more than fifty yards from home. I shudder when I think of the terror that went through the hearts of those little lost kids before death kindly ended it all.

And grown men ran into the same situation. The editor of our weekly newspaper knew his way around town pretty well—the village was simply a crossroads that for all practical purposes was composed of four blocks. But he got so dust-snarled one afternoon, not a hundred yards from home, that the only two directions he was relatively sure of were *up* and *down*. Only his sense of touch and knowledge of landmarks got him through, quite properly on his knees. Perhaps he, like me in my somewhat similar experience, thought upon Ash Wednesday's solemn warning "Remember, O man, that dust thou art and unto dust shalt thou return."

This editor was the same fellow who once raced a black blizzard at his car's full speed down a straight road, with the storm slowly gaining until it was riding his back bumper as he whirled into his own driveway. I mention this incident because it gives some notion of the speed with which these things could move. The one just alluded to was obviously doing around seventy miles an hour—and that brings up the subject of the physical damage the dusters did.

First, naturally, was the erosion of topsoil. It was fertility centuries deep that went whirling off across the plains, on several occasions to settle in the middle of the Atlantic Ocean, some two or three thousand miles away from home. There were deaths and terrible accidents to be taken into account—like the fellow who impaled himself and his car on the end of a bridge. And then there was general damage to business which, in my day, ground to a standstill for the three long months of the dust-storm period.

When it was possible (where there were relatives "back East" in Wichita or Kansas City), whole families packed up and departed, leaving the man of the house behind to answer the mail. You can imagine the number of dismal poker parties that the residual bachelors must have promoted when they weren't tending to their businesses—which was a great deal of the time because there wasn't any business.

This was not simply because as few people as possible remained in the area. It was also because the region itself became restricted. Suppose, for example, that your livelihood or your responsibility depended on your automobile, as was the case with me and many others in that far-flung land. My parishioners and missions were scattered over an area considerably larger than the state of New Jersey. Oil filters weren't common back then, and I didn't have one on my car during the first couple of storms. After that I didn't have any engine. A mixture of that dust in crankcase oil is probably the finest abrasive known to man. In no time at all it honed out my car's cylinders until I was using a quart of oil every twenty-five miles. So of course I bought a new engine—which produced a little business for the local garage, I will admit. But I figured that bill against the dubious benefits from subsequent trips, and after that I stayed home a great deal of the time. So did lots of other people. It was healthier for the car and healthier for the driver. Put yourself out there, perhaps imagining that you are an insurance salesman—a fairly typical job. Do you think you would take a trip a hundred miles into

26

the country to drum up a little trade? Not unless your own life-insurance premiums are paid, and you love your wife enough to want her to collect on it.

Calling on farmers—the economic backbone of the region—didn't do much good, anyway. They were a bit discouraged, what with their mortgaged land blowing away and their wheat stalks being filed down to the level of the remaining ground, so they were not in a mood to buy. I was on a trip once, just calling on parishioners for general good will, when I came to a place where the farmer and his boys were out unburying their wheat combine. A combine, as you know, is roughly as big as a house, and certainly as big as a summer cottage. This one was buried up to the hilt in drifted dust. I took one look at the heroic labors that were going on to get that bit of massive machinery freed so that it could then be taken apart and thoroughly cleaned and decided it would be more opportune to drop in some other time to inquire about the family's well-being. Maybe on my return swing. At the moment I passed by on the other side—a Biblical maneuver, to be sure, but not an honored one.

The memory of this total experience, then, is what produces my present boredom when friends bemoan the weather. For there are two kinds of bad weather—the merely uncomfortable and the definitely calamitous. Most of our fair country knows only the first variety, and that at rare intervals. For the disastrous kind I will defend the Kansas weather I knew against all comers.

Yes, I know that Florida has its hurricanes (I've been in one) and our West Coast has its earthquakes (ditto), and far be it from me to low-rate either of those horrors. But even of these things one can inquire—do they cover a period of three months, as the Kansas dusters did?

However, even in that beleaguered land the long nightmare finally came to an end, and in typically Kansas fashion. The whole town, my wife and I included, was at the movies one night, watching an excellent and absorbing picture. Then, somewhere along about halfway through the feature, a strange restlessness crept over

27

the audience. Back of us people began to get up and go out. I couldn't imagine what was the matter with them, but there was a stirring in the atmosphere that would not be denied, so we went outside too.

It was raining. It was raining buckets for the first time in years—little children out there had never in their lives seen such a thing before—and we all stood in the lobby a little hysterically to watch it rain. The doctor finally rounded up a few of us and took us to his office for a drink. We had quite a celebration.

And I would not be surprised if all of western Kansas did the same, despite the fact that the state was then nominally dry, alcoholically speaking. I would not be surprised if the next morning's sun rose on one of the largest mass hangovers in the history of this weather-beaten planet. But I would maintain that any and all participants were entirely justified.

THREE

Pop and I

*. . . it's the little things that
can change your whole life.*

Courtesy of Dick and the Holy Ghost, after two years in Kansas and
four in Newark, I served for six years as chaplain (then and forever
after known as "Pop") at a Church boarding school in western
North Carolina, living in the midst of 165 teenage boys twenty-four
hours a day. They were omnipresent to me, and I to them. We were
involved with each other in the classroom, on the athletic field, in
the dining room, in long hours of physical work as they kept the
campus in shape, at parties, at dances, at assemblies, at rehearsals,
at plays, at play, in the dormitories, in the infirmary, in the church,
in meetings of various groups, in extracurricular activity, in solitary
conversations one-on-one as they knelt in the confessional or as we
lounged on the grass under a tree, dissecting the universe. In those
circumstances the wall of partition that can too easily separate
clergy from laity unavoidably crumbled, broke down, eroded away.

To a considerable degree I could not avoid coming to know what they were thinking and entering into their concerns. But let's turn the first person singular over to eighth-grader Robby and thus slip inside his mind:

Pop's a good guy. So when I saw him sitting on the iron bench under the oak tree enjoying the June sunshine—or rather, the shade—I naturally walked over there and sat down beside him.

"How are things, Robby?" he said.

"Not good," I told him. Then, after I had dug my heel around in the dirt for a while, I said, "I suppose I have to go."

"They say it's part of the growing-up process," he admitted.

That's one thing I like about Pop—he usually knows what you're talking about. Right now, for instance, to anybody else I'd have had to explain that there was a school dance that night which Mr. Harper, our headmaster, said we would all attend or else, and of course I didn't want to. Pop knew all that without being told.

"Just exactly what have you got against dances?" he asked me.

Ever since Mr. Harper told us in assembly that we were all expected—now there's a nice way to put it—to be at that dance, I'd been going over my reasons against them, so I could answer that one easily. To some people I could have pointed out that this dance came on the Saturday night before final exams and that there were a few matters of business I could profitably attend to that evening. To these people I could go on to say that, for example, I could spend the evening reading the very book which Pop himself assigned last month and writing the book report on it that had to be in before finals. I could point out that my folks had sent me off to this school to get an education and that they were paying good money for it. So here I was, anxious to get an education by reading a book, and the school itself took up my time so I couldn't.

Unfortunately, I couldn't say all that to Pop. He would just raise his eyebrows at me; he wouldn't even bother to answer in words. One trouble with him is that he knows when you're lying. He even

30

knows when you're trying to lie to yourself, which often a guy himself doesn't know.

So I told him the truth, nearly. I said, "You have to dress up at dances, act polite every minute, and watch what you say at all times. There's a law that at dances you have to be completely uncomfortable for three solid hours."

"Look on the bright side," Pop said. "For instance, there's punch and cookies at dances."

"Who wants punch and cookies?"

"I've known you to," he told me.

"Not at that price," I said.

"What price?" he asked. "Do you mean that alleged discomfort, or do you really mean the price of feminine company?"

I was too unhappy to react, so I only nodded. Pop was right. There are always girls at dances, of course, and girls always bring boys misery. I remember the other dances this year, to all of which we were "expected to go." No matter how early I got to the gymnasium—that's where we hold our dances—somehow I was always the last one to arrive. The rest of the gang had gotten there first and crammed into one corner of the gym like a bunch of chilly chickens, so I had to stand in the outside ring ready for plucking.

Now we've got some pretty good boys at this school—along with some of the other kind, of course. Normally they'll do you a favor if it's not too much trouble, but at dances something happens to them. They get selfish. They won't let you crowd through them into the back row against the solid brick wall. As soon as you start to worm through them, they begin acting ugly, asking who you think you are and what do you think you're doing anyway. They shove you back into the outside row, so when one of the chaperones comes along it's your arm she grabs and it's you she pilots across that big naked floor to introduce to some girl. So there you are in the middle of that monstrous empty floor, stuck.

You're stuck because one of the biggest troubles with girls is that you can't talk to them. With boys, of course, you never have to bother to think what you're going to talk about; you just blurt it out.

Let's say you're walking along with Pop talking about trapping skunks when all of a sudden you feel called upon to comment on the slump the New York Yankees are in. It's perfectly all right because Pop is with you all the way.

This sort of thing cannot be done with girls. You can't even talk with them about mild matters like marbles or archery because girls are not athletically inclined. Now I don't mean to say that archery is for the birds; in fact, I really like it. Pop coaches the school's archery club I belong to, so I know a few things about it, including how hard it is to shoot a perfect end—which I've never done. My point is that girls wouldn't even know what a perfect end is, so conversation about one is out of the question.

For all I know girls can talk only about dresses, which is not my best subject. Pictures in magazines give me the impression that girls curl up on divans, call each other up on the telephone, and spend the entire day talking about dresses and hats. I really wouldn't know. What I do know is that when one of the chaperones grabs your arm and pilots you across that big naked floor to introduce you to some girl, you've had it. There is nothing to talk about. Have you ever danced an entire sweaty evening without saying one word, until you want to shriek?

I started to think about all that, and as soon as I started to think, I started to sweat, long before the actual misery began. "Pop," I said, "what can you *say* to a girl when you dance with her?"

"Why not say something she'd like to hear?" he suggested.

"Now what in the world would one of them like to hear?" I asked him. He wasn't any help at all, and I never did find out anything from him because just then Fink came along to join us on the bench. To be fair to Pop I'd better say that he doesn't often let you down like that.

When Fink sat down, Pop said to him, "We were talking about the dance tonight. That reminds me—do you have any new records I haven't heard?"

Fink is really a platter jockey; probably no one in the world has as many records as he has. Sometimes I go to his room before lights

32

out to listen to them. So do lots of other guys. Up on the wall over his desk Fink's got a map of the United States, with pins in it to show where all the big bands are playing at that time. He really knows his bands.

Fink closed his eyes and leaned his head back. "Have I got one!" he said. He was talking soft and far away. "This is only the best record that's ever been made. This is *my* record." Then he came to. "Let's go over and hear it," he said.

"Come along, Robby," Pop said to me. So I went. When we got to the room Fink put his record on.

Now I don't know too much about bands. This record had all sorts of queer sounds in it, and sometimes even I could tell what was making the sounds because Fink would put his hand out into the air and run his fingers up and down when the piano was playing, or up in front of his face in different positions when it was a trumpet or clarinet or saxophone. He reached out to beat the drums too—there were lots of drums in this record—but of course I know what drums are. To me it always was more fun to watch Fink than it was to hear his music because, as I said, I don't know much about bands.

"That's good, is it?" Pop said when the record was finally over. He sounded as if he didn't know much about music either.

"Good?" Fink raised his eyes to the angels in heaven. "Look—can you kiss a trumpet like that?"

Pop admitted he couldn't.

"Ah, that trumpet!" said Fink, dreamy again. "And that whole band! Still, who couldn't build a band around that trumpet?"

"They won't have music like that tonight," Pop said. "Of course, they will have girls."

"Yes," said Fink, and you could tell he was pleased at the thought. "Ah, yes."

"I've noticed you get along acceptably with them," Pop went on.

"A wolf," said Fink, adjusting his tie.

"How do you do it?" Pop asked him. He sat down and lit his pipe.

"You're kidding me!"

"Not a bit." Pop blew a smoke ring. "I'm really serious."

"Well, Pop, I'll tell you," said Fink. "I guess the average person's big trouble is when he meets a new girl for the first time. He gets sort of paralyzed in the presence. Of course, after he gets to know them there's no difficulty. No difficulty at all."

"Never mind that part," Pop told him. "Let's get back to the beginning."

"Well, here's what I do," Fink said. "Of course, you understand that the *way* it's done is the most important thing, and that's hard to teach in so many words. You'd better watch me in action tonight, live. Anyway, after I've cut in on some lucky chick and we've gone a few steps, I say, 'My, you dance well.' Of course I step back a little bit to give them the old look. You know—as if I was really living for the first time. That breaks the ice. I mean it really fractures it. Then I go on, always talking about *them*. That's my little Open Sesame. I say things like—'Where's your home, honey?'; and 'What school do you go to, sugar?'; and 'In what fortunate place do you spend the summers?'" Fink was ticking these things off on his fingers, and you can bet I was too. "Then I always make sure to say, somewhere along the line, 'That's a mighty pretty dress you're wearing, angel.' Ah me, how they love it."

"It sounds as if it might be effective," Pop admitted. "Somewhere in the answers to those questions you ought to find something to talk about."

"The fellow who doesn't ought to crawl back into his deep freeze and read Thoreau. With a bright boy it simply can't fail."

"Do you mind running over all that again?" Pop asked him. "I'd like to get it straight."

So Fink went over his line once more, with Pop following closely. I only hope he learned as much as I did. Because, believe me, that conversation changed my entire life, including my ideas about dances and girls. I often wonder what my life would have been like if Pop hadn't happened to say "Come along" to me when he got up from the bench with Fink. I'd certainly never have met Betty.

34

Things like that make you realize how it's the little things that can change your whole life.

You know, before I went to that dance I never thought that one girl's name was any different from another's. In my stupidity I had never realized that Betty is an especially nice name. Now that word makes me feel funny inside. I wrote Betty on my algebra book the morning after the dance. I felt good just seeing it there; I felt good just carrying that book around, which is saying a good deal about an algebra book.

But about the dance. I practiced what I learned from Fink while he was teaching Pop, until I got it perfect. Then when the evening rolled around, I felt secure, if you know what I mean. I hardly held back at all when a chaperone came up to take my arm and lead me across the dance floor. Even when I started to dance with this utterly strange girl in the foamy light-blue dress, it wasn't bad at all.

In two minutes it was a whole lot better than that. When I got to "What do you do in the summers?", Betty told me that her father ran an archery camp in Vermont and that of course she spent her summers there.

Right in the middle of the floor I backed off to really look at this girl in the blue dress. I hardly noticed the half-dozen couples who bumped into us although from certain remarks I am certain they noticed me. "Then I'm sure you shoot a bow yourself," I said.

"Oh, certainly," she said. "I've been shooting for years."

"Well," I said. "Well, I'll be durned."

We were still sort of standing there, with guys making observations all around us, when somebody cleared his throat right behind Betty. I knew that throat, so I didn't need to look up to realize that Mr. Harper had danced up with Mrs. Harper, and that he was giving me that look. We danced away from there pretty fast.

"What do you like best about archery?" I asked Betty as soon as it was safe to begin talking again.

She didn't answer for a while. Then she said, "Well, I like the kind of people who go in for it—the world champion is an especially nice person; you'd like him. And the targets do look beautiful on

35

the green meadow, with the mountains behind them in the distance." She stopped a minute, and I was sorry because Betty undoubtedly has the nicest, most tinkling voice in the world, especially when you compare it with the horrible croaks I'd been hearing all year in our dorm. Then she wrinkled her freckled nose—just watching that sent chills down my spine—and said, "You won't think I'm too competitive?"

I told her I couldn't imagine anything bad about her at any time.

"I like to be in close competition on Target One as a tournament nears its end. You know. You've been shooting all day under the hot sun. You're tired, but you know you can't let down for a second because your opponent is the State Champion. You're two points ahead, on the last end of the last round, and your opponent shoots a perfect end. You know you have to do the same or—"

"You're telling me something that actually happened, aren't you?" I said. "And you put all your own arrows in the gold too, didn't you?"

Betty wrinkled up her nose again. "It isn't important," she said. "But it's fun."

The rest of that dance is blurred in my memory. Oh, I remember parts, like meeting Pop at the punchbowl where he and I and Betty chatted along like old friends. Pop seemed to like Betty, too.

Unfortunately I also remember some times when other fellows cut in on me while Betty and I were dancing.

Still, most of the rest of the evening is a blur, except of course the most important part. That came when the dance was all over before it hardly got started and we were walking along under the stars to the bus that all the girls came in. It was while we were walking along and Betty was saying yes, she'd love to come to the graduation dance with me, that my hand happened to brush against hers. That part is strictly none of your business.

FOUR

The Home Place

*. . . our preference was for homespun
pleasures and broken bones.*

When I myself was Robby's age, our family moved from downtown
rented quarters out to our very own, our new and permanent, home
at the city limits of Summit, New Jersey, where I was to live the so-
important formative years. To be perfectly accurate, in that long-ago
summer of 1920 half of our family moved into the new place while
the other half took up residence in its guest cottage.

We did not thus separate because some of us were mad at the
others. The temporary split-up occurred because our new house was
really very old (circa 1814), quite small, and in need of improvements as well as enlargement. While the latter was in process, we
three boys lived happily in an old chicken coop up on the hill. Our
small sister, who was a girl and therefore did not in that long-ago era
enjoy equal rights with us males, had to live in the main house with
our parents. We boys did join the others for meals and at chores and

at church until work at the house was "completed," if I may use that word loosely. On Christmas Eve, as it happened, the family was reunited under one roof.

One of our chores during the five months of separation was carrying water, for the manor house had no more running water than did our guest cottage. Running water requires plumbing, and while that was being installed, we lugged our supply in pails from a bountiful and lovely spring nestled in the roots of a beech tree a hundred yards away. When your water arrives on foot, you're careful with it. Even after the plumbers had connected us to the town's main, in-house water was the extent of our newfound luxury for quite a while. I realize now that available funds couldn't be stretched to include a septic tank, so for a long time we had to make do with a gravel-filled hole in the ground, only adequate to handle limited sink water. In any case, our bathroom left something to be desired for more than a year. During that interval, one of its prime facilities was located thirty yards outside the back door, over in a clump of rhododendron next to our cornfield. It was a pleasant enough place during the summers—one day while I was dawdling in it, a herd of a dozen deer drifted by—but in winter a visit there was undertaken for urgent daytime business only. I never used it on winter nights, and my guess is that nobody else in our family did either.

Throughout that same long interlude our winter bathing—the really thorough kind preparatory for church on Sunday—was done regularly every Saturday night by turns beginning with the youngest—Sis—in a galvanized tub before the hearthfire. Bath water was heated on our kerosene stove and, after it was used, poured on the ground rather than down the sink into our dubious dry well, so on many counts we were sparing about quantity. Even with due care six serial baths took quite a lot of water as well as considerable time. However, there is nothing like a hot bath followed by a brisk toweling before a blazing fire in an otherwise chilly room and then by encasement in warmed flannel pajamas. After that came the final dash to an icy bed heavy with blankets and a down comforter.

38

On cowardly nights you assumed the fetal position, with tentative inchings of your toes down into the absolute zero beyond them. When brave, you warmed your bed all at once, flat out.

Our bathing room was chilly on the side of you away from the hearthfire—how your body steamed!—for the simple reason that our whole house was. Always. All over. Without any turning down of thermostats. As a matter of fact we had no thermostat. There was indeed a heating device in the place—the plumbers had installed that too—but coal cost money, so the fire in our furnace was always banked low. On special occasions, like ten below zero outside, mother would peer into it a dozen times a day to see if it was actually burning at all.

That heating system merits brief description. It was a single-pipe hot-water rig—gravity type, without circulating pump—installed about a hundred years after the house had been built. Hence its vast pipes were as much out in the open as its huge radiators. The plumbers hung those enormous iron pipes up near the ceilings on chains from the joists, like a skeleton outside its body, and there they remain to this day, high-tech and very mod. Warm water will flow through them when you have a fire in the furnace, but they are not things of beauty in my eyes. The best I can say is that they're different. Even in our high-tech era you do not see their like every day.

Our furnace itself had been installed in the kitchen—an unhandy place, but the house had no basement. It didn't even have a crawl space beneath it. My brothers and I scrambled all over that house, you may be sure, but none of us ever got under it. There simply wasn't any "under." The place had been built Termite Heaven, right on the ground. It still stands solidly and defiantly there, a unique, a lovely, and a thoroughly comfortable house now. In an irrelevant aside I report that it sold, quite a few years ago, for $100,000 with a seventy-five-foot lot. My parents had bought it and five acres of ground for forty-five hundred dollars. I suspect that they knew from the start what they could bring to pass with steady purpose, hard work, some scrimping and even some cramping, along the way. The vision undoubtedly helped keep them warm.

But if our parents were indeed looking forward to a future alleviation of lean times, we children were busily living in the present. Hindsight assures me that we lived close to the bone, but at the time frugality was the only lifestyle we knew and therefore was the only one there was. We perceived it as being the very nature of reality, and we reveled in it. We were also enriched by it.

We everlastingly learned, early on, to be economical without being mean; to be flagrantly outgoing and yet not waste a thing. Without any moralizing parental lectures we learned to enjoy things simple and at hand. To savor life itself rather than its incidental trappings. Even to be, rather than to seem. Certainly to want (in one sense of the word) and to work toward achieving desire. Finally, to lack without sense of loss.

Also, to defer or to improvise. You should have seen some of our homemade gadgets and toys. Horrible bows and worse arrows. Awkward swords and shields. Deadly slingshots. Boomerangs that failed to work. High-jump stands. Wagons. Archetypal skateboards. Huts. Rabbit traps. Catapults with which to demolish, at great labor, a fort constructed at great labor. Arc lights. Telegraph instruments. Radios of various complexities. For lack of these fantastic and primitive artifacts the Smithsonian is not impoverished, but no museum could have afforded to buy them anyway. Their value was beyond price. In designing and constructing them we joined the human race; became kin to Edison and the Wright brothers; were nudged above our animal nature into a world of consciousness and creativity.

This seems a good place to pause and assure you that our parents had selected the Home Place with great care and supremely well, not because it was within their means but because it was located at the exact center of the universe. Its own ample acres included garden space and yielded firewood, cherries, walnuts, hickory nuts, apples, quinces, plums, blackberries, currants, rhubarb, and asparagus from the moment we moved in. Eighty yards away from this navel of the cosmos, across aptly named Division Avenue, that boundary line between town and county, shooting firecrackers became legal. Half a mile farther distant was the Big Hill, ideal for coasting in the winter and unvisited by any automobiles to make that sport more hazardous than we could manage unassisted. Just above the Big Hill lay an abortive golf course, its cleared and rolling fairways abandoned in midterm by a bankrupt developer. In decent winters a series of sunlit days followed by snapping cold nights created on those snow-covered fairways a crust thick enough to support an elephant and froze the ice in a water-hole sufficiently solid to hold up the rest of its family. We could boom hundreds of yards down a clear glass mountain toward that pond, hurtle twenty feet or so through the air courtesy of its upthrusting near bank, and with skillful diligence avoid disaster at its far, alas nearly vertical, bank. On one such run Mother was, unfortunately, neither skillful nor diligent. When she hit the far side of that pond straight on, going sixty, her sled stopped right now, but she didn't. She was shot off her catapult as from a cannon, head first into that cement crust, breaking her nose and acquiring a pair of gaudy shiners. Socially, but fortunately not otherwise, she was incapacitated for the better part of a month afterwards. However, Mother had neither time, inclination, or wherewithal to mingle much in society, any more than the rest of us did. Our preference, as should by now be clear, was for homespun pleasures and broken bones. My left arm became a casualty, along with my barrel staves, on our ski jump. We had been lazy and built it in that cornfield, which was really too steep a place for corn but proved to be insufficiently so for a decent ski jump. I sort of dripped off the end of it, headfirst. We built a faster jump the next winter, in a more remote but better place. One learns, if one lives.

Over the hill from our Ground Zero was a secret lake which civilization discovered only a decade or so later. In its heyday of our private possession we swam in it all summer long; in winter we wore it to a frazzle with all-day hockey games. Occasionally we enjoyed the use of a genuine hockey puck, acquired at Christmas. Usually it would last us most of the morning before we lost it down a hole in the ice, but we went merrily on with the game, using some sort of substitute puck.

From time to time we went down a hole in the ice ourselves, most times near shore at the lake's feeder streams while in hot pursuit of an imperiled puck. The water was frigid, naturally, and one got out of there as fast as he could, but the little incident didn't dampen our fun. The victim just skated around for a while to remain flexible while his clothes froze—which was soon—and after that he was cozily incased in windproof armor plate. Years later people would make similar windbreakers the easy way, from plastic.

But let's get back inside our house where it's warmer, although not much. In my youth, as stated above and for the reason there stated, our Goldberg climate modifier released BTUs grudgingly. The stove itself did provide solid support for a ceiling-high stack of oat-sprouting trays—we were in the egg business, and the theory was that our Leghorns needed winter greens. Those oats had the best of it, there close to the heart of things. The far-ranging pipes got what was left over. They never actually froze because my father saw to it that a tepid stream drifted along through their serpentine course, and neither did we. We just never, or hardly ever, were really warm save in front of our fireplace. "Put another sweater on" is a family expression to this day. When you say that, smile.

Our place did include some acres of forest, so my brothers and I were able to maintain a huge woodlot near the kitchen door for a span of a decade and more. In the process we wore out a couple of crosscut saws, countless wedges, and half a dozen axes. All of us still love to cut wood, and continually do so. My oldest brother, now pushing eighty-two, is the worst of our lot. He supplies his whole Connecticut neighborhood with firewood, for pleasure, and won't even travel without basic equipment—chainsaw, axe, rope—in the trunk of his car. You never can tell when you'll need them, he says, and generally he manages to need them. Last Christmas, for example, on a holiday visit with his grandchildren he cut down four great trees to celebrate the occasion. Once again, the habits and philosophy acquired in youth die hard, if at all.

Now that I have begun to wander from strict chronology, let me really get lost in time by harking back, and then forward, to the time of the Great Depression, still in the same old Home Place. Obviously we youngsters had by then long since grown up some, worked our ways through colleges somehow, gotten jobs somewhere, and in due course married. Then along came the thirties, that national night when no man could work. One after the other, but two by two because accompanied by spouses this time around, we crept back home to roost, to lick our wounds, and to scurry in all directions looking for gainful employment. In fairly short order our Homestead, our Ark of Salvation, was bursting with ten of us—two more than rode out the storm in Noah's time.

Our ark still had only one bathroom, all of it indoors by this time and attached to an actual sewer. Nevertheless, with ten healthy people waiting in line, even this splendor called for dispatch and nice timing. We men frequently shaved simultaneously—we never thought to reinvent beards—and sometimes one wasn't wholly sure whose face he was barbering. Our several wives would be down in the one-woman kitchen at the same time, making sandwich lunches for us to take to such work as we might have located or dreamed up for that day. Their turn to get ready to report at such jobs as they may have found would come later. (Query: how went matutinal matters in the ménage of Noah, Shem, Ham, and Japeth?)

Between the ten of us we did manage to scrape together dimes and even occasional dollars—for a spell there we went into the firewood business, what else?—during those grim months. We cultivated a vast garden, in soil enriched for a decade with chicken manure and fertile beyond belief, we ate fairly regularly, we paid the utility bills, and we kept the house warm a good deal of the time. So for deeper insight into the Great Depression I will have to take you down our road to a neighbor (let's call him Dan) who was finding things much harder than we were. He had a wife, five children—a new generation of our old gang—and no job at all.

The electric company saved Dan financial embarrassment by cutting off its service to him. So did the gas company. Likewise the oil people. Telephone, the same. In a situation like this you conserve water, and your house, by shutting it off at the main and draining the place. You trek to that same old spring or up to our house with pails for your daily needs. You build an outhouse in your spare time, of which you have plenty, and with the help of willing neighbors of whom you have many. You install a wood-burning stove in your kitchen, and when push comes to shove in the eating line, you cook twenty gallons of oatmeal at one crack and keep it on the back burner, ready and waiting for hungry stomachs at any hour. Oatmeal is tasty with brown sugar and butter, when you have any.

You also enjoy a good life through it all, thanks to past experience with the nature of reality. On that familiar old ground we resumed our familiar old lifestyle, throwing in a few new adult wrinkles like evenings of bridge at Dan's by candlelight, wearing overcoats. Dummy fed the hearthfire. On really splendid occasions we had the makings of cigarettes, rolled on that little tin gizmo.

Our afflicted nation made it through those good old bitter days, some say the better for the experience. You may be happy to hear that our family made it through very nicely, and so did Dan's. Scattered to the four winds now in retirement, we all remain welded together in unbreakable unity. The Great Depression wasn't all bad.

Hold your fire for a minute before you shoot. Far be it from me to say, or in any way imply, that the deep misery of our Great Depression was visited upon the earth in order to stir up a few fleas. Also far be it from me to say, or to imply, that our modern world might benefit from a rerun of that Depression. One could hope for less radical therapy. Certainly I wish to be excused if ever they play it again. Once was enough, and to spare.

Yet if in the Infinite Wisdom a salutary bomb had to be dropped upon us all in the thirties, its lesser side-effects might as well include taking account of a flea. That is to say, during and because of the Depression I gratefully plunged into several different lines of work, but none beckoned onward to a fulfilling career. After a while I began to glimpse the truth that when you are on the wrong road it becomes an ever-narrowing path that finally peters out completely, leaving you lost, once again, in the woods.

So in a way I appreciate the Great Depression because I owe everything to it. First of all it stopped me in my tracks. Then it forced me to think, to face truths about myself, and ultimately to take steps in a new direction. Thus it set me on my correct course—the one I had so long avoided—whereupon doors began to open on oiled hinges and have kept on swinging open ever since. But we need a bit more background before we get into all that.

FIVE

Collectors' Items

We Episcopalians have a lot of religion,
but no morals at all.

While I was sweeping the patio of our retirement place this morning, the small boy from next door drifted across, trailing a length of
rope that I should have immediately realized was not just a length of
rope.

"Do you know how to make a lasso?" he challenged me.

I told him that it had been a long time and that I was afraid I
had forgotten, so he showed me. He also showed me how to twirl it
around and then throw it, snaring a fence post. When he wandered
off in search of bigger, possibly live, game, he took his lasso with
him, but he left behind a magic carpet on which to fly back across
the years. He himself won't want it for a long time. When he does it
will be readily available, and in a brand new model, custom-built
exclusively for him, as mine is for me and yours is, or will be, for you.

In connection with my past I used to regret, among more

important matters, that I had failed to save some of the common things of my boyhood—a Charles Evans Hughes campaign button, a set of baseball cards, some marbles and a boxwood top, an Ingersoll watch complete with its fob, a menu from Delmonico's, the playbill of *Lady Be Good* autographed by Gershwin and Astaire, the ten-dollar gold pieces my godfather gave me every Christmas and birthday for a decade or so. (The trouble there was that we had to eat them as they came in, first having turned them into money.)

I used to regret that my parents had not done the same—saved a few everyday items and passed the loot down to me for its intrinsic and reminiscence values. I would now have a fine collection of antique milk bottles, early Mason jars, sleeve garters, carpet beaters, programs from the Hippodrome, a complete file of *St. Nicholas Magazine*, an unusual old music cabinet, and some original General Motors stock.

Above all I used to regret that my grandparents hadn't employed 20-20 foresight and saved for me their Magic Lantern, their stereopticon with all its slides, a set of carpenter's tools with wooden-bodied planes, a butter churn, a first edition signed by Mark Twain, and that lake in northern New Jersey which one grandfather sold, after his children grew up and were done with it, for four thousand dollars complete with summer cottage. That property is now worth untold millions.

But it came to my attention that I would have had trouble storing some of those never-assembled things and paying the taxes on the others. And after all the members of the generations before mine had in their turn been gathered to their fathers, my regrets began to run in another direction. I could no longer sit at their feet and listen to their tales about life and people Back Then. It would be impossible, henceforth, to fill in the historical gaps that I had lacked wit to query them about when they and their memories were ready to hand. With that vault of treasure locked shut and its key thrown away, I would be to that degree always impoverished.

Naturally I had picked up, along the way, some smatterings about my family and its history. Ancestor John Howland, presumably while sober, fell off the Mayflower in a storm and saved himself by grabbing a trailing rope. For a while in that tossing sea the lives of all my kin, not to mention my own, hung by a thread. Happily, Howland was hauled back on board, so a lot of us were enabled to fight in the Revolutionary War, on the winning side. Among them were a general or so and a lieutenant about whom legend, and possibly history, avers that he donated (he submitted a bill for it later) his blue cloak as material for an American flag to be stitched together by one Betsy Ross, an ancestress of my wife. Obviously it was foreordained that she and I should ultimately get together.

A bit later on in time the Swartout brothers, from whom our family gets its oversized Dutch noses, dug those futile drainage ditches in the Jersey Meadows which were still visible when I was a young man, and maybe still are. Sam Swartout, a buddy of Aaron Burr and admired by Andrew Jackson, who appointed him Collector of the Port of New York, is alleged to have absconded with a million dollars of the Port Authority's money, but I have been unable to trace where he may have stashed it. Ignorance about one's family can be so frustrating.

My great-grandfather was ordained deacon and priest by Jackson Kemper, Episcopal Bishop of All Outdoors, in Wisconsin in the 1850s. I have his ordination certificates in Kemper's handwriting which so testify, but there is a yawning gap between the days and the likes of Sam Swartout and great-grandfather Edmunds. Somebody in the family must have been doing something odd, or hilarious, or even significant, during that interval, but nobody told me a word about it.

After I came on the scene, I never had the sense to ask my great-grandfather's son, also a clergyman, who will appear in these pages and in whose then-small person the Patriarch brought our family back East, about his reactions to the Civil War, the assassination of Lincoln, and other commonplaces of his youth. I do know that my other grandfather and his son, my father, were stuck for a couple of cold and hungry days and nights in a stalled train during the Blizzard of '88, but again there are vast gaps. Even the chronology is elusive.

49

Grandfather Webbe may have spent that chilling interlude second-guessing his rejection of the offer to co-found and become treasurer of the Prudential (or was it the Metropolitan?) Insurance Company. The risky opportunity had appealed to him, but he had a young wife, two babies, and a secure job at the time, so he took the safe course.

I have been told that one of my grandmothers had her appendix removed by the surgeon (McBurney?) whose name is still associated with this procedure, and I do hope the historic scar was acquired under an anesthetic, but I was never informed about that. I am aware that my father once played the world chess champion—or was it the American champion?—to a draw. I am in possession of a few other semi-facts of that sort, but I haven't the least idea, to take an example, whether any of our clan cavorted around with Teddy Roosevelt or whether they all despised him.

I don't even know why my parents moved to Canada for a spell when I was about five years old. Why came they back, to own and operate that motion-picture non-palace, the Bandbox, in Newark, New Jersey? I don't know. I only know I was a popular young man then, at least on Saturdays, for on that day a friend could accompany me, for free, to witness the *Perils of Pauline* and the adventures of Eddie Polo. What is the real story about that dotty great-aunt who lived for years locked up on the third floor out in Denver, and does that sort of thing run in the family? What were my parents' memories of World War I? (Listen, my children, and you shall hear mine: I remember standing in line on a bitter cold night waiting my turn for a hundred-pound bag of coal, which I then hauled home on my sled; and saving peach-pits, I think to be ground up for use in gas-mask filters. There you have my World War I, whole and entire.)

Next time around I may be more searching in my questions to the Old Ones; more careful about gathering together and saving these true collector's items. They don't take up any storage room, nor are they subject to annual tax. Moth and rust can't lay a glove on them. They just give one's being an important extra dimension; they put one more deeply into the flow of things.

But, then, I might not. Certainly when my children, grand-children, and great-grandchild gather around the glowing hearth this Christmas, I am not going to ask them to hold still for five minutes while I recount a personal recollection or two. Nobody wants to go poking around in the ashes of the past when we all will be having such a lively time being together in the present. And that's the real way a person builds up the store of memories which do so much for his identity.

I have come to realize that my elders knew this and acted on it. They doled out enough for the next generation to go on, but didn't bury it under too much. They were indeed concerned to provide a continuum, to set a solid base under my feet. But they wanted me to use that platform as a launching pad into the future. Their major bequest was a lifetime supply of faith and hope, the best possible endowment for the clergyman I would come to be.

Since I propose to spare my family a gaffer's reminiscences this Christmas, I'd like to record here, somewhat for antiquarian pur-poses but with a far more important point really in mind, a few notes on the youthful lifestyle of my generation, now so rapidly passing away. About the time when kings go forth to battle—about the time when kite-season came and still comes in early spring—we brought our cache of marbles out of safekeeping. Kites continue to fly, but marbles don't seem to be in fashion any more. I do readily find them in the stores, where I buy them for slingshot ammunition in a futile effort to keep the squirrels out of my cornpatch, but I never see the kids hunkered down on the muddy ground using them as God intended. Marbles certainly meant a lot to us when youngsters, providing a long season for the exercise of skill and altercation. We did occasionally go in for Duck-on-the-Rock, Kick-the-Can, or Kick-the-Stick, for games of tag and hide-and-seek, as soon as winter's snows were gone, but the various marble games were our really steady fare until the baseball season came along. I wish I could remember all the games and all the rules.

51

By the way, whatever became of rolling a hoop with a stick or a pusher, of playing hopscotch and jacks (essentially games for girls, but boys could occasionally indulge without losing face if they were careful to exhibit an amused superiority), and of tops? Admittedly, I don't frequent hobby shops in these last days, but I have not so much as seen a top for years in any store, let alone spinning merrily on the street or sidewalk. Our enjoyment of them included trying to split somebody else's spinning top by hitting it with one of our own. Cheap softwood ones split readily, provided you could hit them in the center. Lucky or affluent kids owned a stout hardwood top, itself nearly impervious to damage but a deadly weapon for destroying lesser ones.

Baseball, given the scarcity of players out our way, was generally one-o-cat. In summer we played it all day long on our private diamond across the road, where the manicured mansions now stand and which became a football gridiron in the fall. Even as a boy I wondered how we knew so infallibly when one sport's season yielded properly to the next; when bat and glove were to be put aside and the pigskin hunted down and pumped up. We lacked any Stonehenge, but we knew with certainty. Possibly our very genes and chromosomes are programmed for kites, marbles, and tops in the spring; for baseball, swimming, and catching fireflies in the summer; for football, hunting, and gathering nuts in the fall; for hockey, basketball, sledding, and skiing in the winter.

Indoor games—bridge and the like—could acceptably be played at any time, I believe, although winter was the truly proper one. (Be it recorded that my wife was raised a Methodist of the strictest sort and never held a playing card in her hand until I came along and corrupted her. We Episcopalians have a lot of religion, but no morals at all.) Certainly my grandparents played whist at any season. My parents progressed to an offshoot of that game, named auction bridge. Only in our own time came the ultimate transitions to contract and duplicate, from Culbertson to Goren and all the others.

However, as youngsters we mostly played lesser card games—pinochle, Liverpool rummy, hearts. In fact I went off to college not really knowing how to play bridge, but under the illusion that I did, and was a pariah until that character defect was corrected. Now I have come full circle, back to Liverpool rummy and hearts again, playing the latter without mercy and for blood when the grandchildren come on a visit.

Parcheesi was the board game *par excellence* before Monopoly came along. My generation may even rank it as a classic, along with chess and checkers. Memory seems to say that such games were less ephemeral then than now. Certainly we got long years of pleasure out of our Parcheesi, our Tinkertoys, our Erector Set. We didn't discard the latter for some later rage, some Johnny-come-lately, batteries not included. Santa Claus simply brought more erector components, with which we joyfully constructed more complicated contraptions, powered by rubber bands.

In the infancy of radio and the nonexistence of television, parlor games, such as charades, came into play when the gang assembled on dark and stormy nights. In our league Post Office and Spin-the-Bottle were sissy affairs indulged in, with manly distaste, only when some silly female from the outside gave a party. Our group of boys and girls went in more for stunts and contests. Possibly we'd get involved in "Simon Says" for a while. Then we'd send one person out, say to the kitchen—he would be in cahoots, in any of several ways, with a crony remaining in the living room. We would choose one of the eight or ten people remaining in the living room, call back the kitchen-boy, and he would unerringly give you the name of the selected person.

Now here's a strange experience: on one occasion, after that game had palled, we decided to see if it could be done without chicanery. I did it easily, time after time. The gang lined up in front of the fireplace with their backs to me, each one of them concentrating mightily on the name they had selected, unknown to me. I would run slowly over the names in my mind, and soon one would begin to stand out; would begin to glow, as it were. It was always the right one, until at last there came a time when I could not make a choice between two equally prominent names. After I admitted I was licked, stating the two names I couldn't choose between, it turned out that there had been confusion about the person selected. Half the group had been concentrating on one, half on the other, of my two names. On that note we quit playing; we never tried the stunt again. There were plenty of other games, tricks, puzzles, riddles, feats of strength, balance, and dexterity to keep us going and let us show off.

When the gang was not around or when a solitary mood struck, my generation practiced on the piano, fiddled with a stamp or butterfly collection, did a lot of reading. In our house this was pretty much confined to the classics. Our bookcases were filled with them, so that is what we read. I don't remember any feeling of loss, or even of great bafflement, because of the limitation. To be sure I see more in Cinderella, Theseus, Alice, Dorothy, Huck Finn, Robinson Crusoe, Kim, Hiawatha, Jim Hawkins, David Copperfield, and Don Quixote now than I did then, but we hit it off adequately on first acquaintance. In fact, I think I was in my early teens before I realized, with some shock, that books were still being written and that people were reading them. My first reaction to the news was one of some resentment toward these upstart modern authors. Who did they think they were? Besides, I hadn't yet had time to read the hundreds of already written books.

We have now reached the deferred and promised point of this chapter. It has taken a while to get here because I have been enjoying the trip down memory lane, as I hope you have too. Yet it has all been a leading-up to the truth that preparation for priesthood begins far back in youth, possibly even as far back as God indicated to Jeremiah when He ordained him a prophet to the nations: "Before I formed thee in the belly I knew thee." However that may be, strewn across one's early years are little telltale signs indicative of later vocation. The developing youngster is unaware of them until from the vantage point of later life he can look back and discern something of an emerging pattern. Observant parents and grandparents, however, note them in the process.

I see now, for example, some basic differences between my elder brother and myself as we lived the same life doing the same things. From the beginning I was essentially the Platonist, he the Aristotelian. It pleased and satisfied something in me to dream up a concept or a caper. My brother was somewhat impatient of anything as vague as a mere idea; he was not satisfied until he had fabricated it, brought it down to earth in a specific contraption. I hasten to say that both of us were sufficiently comfortable on either side of the fence; he was just more truly at home over there while I was more delighted over here. To me the big question was Why. What fascinated him was How. I was the more interested in people; he, in things. On rainy days I would be apt to be up in our room reading. He might be out in the shed tinkering. Or I would stay after school to practice my part in the operetta while he went home to sharpen our crosscut saw. Of course, my favorite academic subjects were English and languages while his were math and science. I was *en rapport* with our clergyman grandfather; my brother with our accountant-treasurer-businessman one.

I repeat that it is untrue to state these things as though they were in contrasting black and white. In actuality, they were shades of grey. Nevertheless, as has also been stated, our parents readily observed the different tones, which is one thing good parents are for. In due course they steered my brother toward Lehigh University, where he prepared for his fulfilled life as a mechanical engineer. Contrariwise, when my time came, they suggested that I consider a liberal arts college like Amherst or Trinity, possibly wondering what might ultimately be lying in wait for me down that fork in the road. The legal profession? Teaching? Even the ministry?

I too wondered. Plato seemed a bit hazy *vis-à-vis* Aristotle and my admired, down-to-earth brother. So after college was through with me I made a U-turn. I withdrew my applications to law school and seminary, went back to the crossroad, took the other fork, and for a time followed my brother's footsteps along that highway. In short, I tried to become an engineer just like him.

It did not work out. You can't be like somebody else. You have to be you, as I finally learned with the help of the Great Depression.

SIX

The Road Ahead

*. . . you had a choice of lights or locomotion,
but not both at once.*

When I arrived on the scene, upward of seventy-nine years ago, a
few primitive gasoline and electric buggies were chugging or gliding
around, warily observed by prescient horses. I drowsed through all
that. By the time my eyes were really open, the Automobile Age
had burst fully upon us. Gentlemen raised their hats and bowed as
ladies, guiding electrics by a tiller held in white-gloved hands,
whispered by en route to the regular meeting of the Fortnightly
Club. We young boys hanging around the blacksmith's on our
meander home from school unerringly identified at a glance the
passing Oldsmobile, White, Pierce-Arrow, Marmon, Studebaker,
Hupmobile, Franklin, Packard, or any of the others. As the dust
settled we argued about each car's strong points, shortcomings, and
mythology—like the allegation that a Stanley Steamer's top speed
was absolutely limitless, but nobody would ever dare drive one wide-

open; or that the hood of a Rolls Royce was locked down at the factory so that no unauthorized mechanic could tinker with the jeweled perfection of its motor.

This milieu which my generation took for granted as its birthright hit our elders, reared on horse and buggy, with revolutionary shock. My father, and his father, never would learn how to drive. To the end of their days they made do with bicycles, trains, trolleys, ultimately buses, and always their own pairs of legs—possibilities now being rediscovered. My other grandfather, however—he who in his childhood had skipped outside to witness the battle of Gettysburg and had been curious about a lot of newfangled things ever since—eagerly embraced this latest development in his seventies. The Commonwealth of Massachusetts, then lenient in these matters, duly certified him fit to drive an automobile. When he came home from that successful exam he rolled into his garage, erstwhile a shed, hauled back on the steering wheel, hollered "Whoa!", and instantly invented the carport in one splintering crash. Later he volunteered to teach my grandmother how to drive, but she declined. As a matter of fact, she wasn't all that wild about letting him take her for a Sunday afternoon's drive.

My own generation could handle anything on wheels and at opportunity did. Probably in the majority of cases nobody had taught us how. Driver training was decades in the future. We just picked up our skill, if such it was, by observation, osmosis, and surreptitious practice. For several years before my mother at last acquired her first car our neighbor kept an early Ford and an equally classic Buick stabled in his cavernous barn—barns came before garages and were standing there ready and waiting. I gave myself driver education in and around that arena on discreet occasions, so I was all ready and waiting too. My wife tells me that she, also aged eleven, learned to drive in a cemetery, weaving in and out among the headstones. One way or another we kids knew all about standard shift, Buick shift, Dodge shift, Reo's single-pedal clutch-and-brake combination, and of course Ford's three pedals before we could distinguish between dinner forks, salad forks, and other such trifles. Motivation is a mighty force.

Driving around a pasture, and especially a cemetery, was excellent preparation for taking to our rudimentary roads with their sharp unbanked curves, their thank-you-ma'ams, their washboard surface, their dust or mud at the weather's whim. A nationwide road-building rush-job did spring up in the twenties, not a minute too soon— cars were rolling off the assembly lines with no place to go— but for a while all that new raw earth only made matters worse. To be sure, early automobile designers sagely provided ample road clearance—a Model-T driver, supremely, sat up there regally enthroned—but it was never enough to prevent evisceration. Tearing off the muffler on iron ruts after a March thaw-and-freeze was common, and I was once disemboweled of a gas tank under those circumstances. (Not in a Ford, where the driver sat on the tank. This would have involved a disemboweling indeed.) Even under the best climatic conditions a driver venturing beyond city limits carried emergency equipment like towrope, shovel, and axe; expected to use them; would have to use them. Local knowledge about grades, curves, shoulders, ditches, washouts, cul-de-sacs, and omnipresent detours kept us from some occasions of grief. No informed motorist would ever drive us all the way home, particularly at night. We lived two miles out of town, on a road God had forgotten and the county remembered only occasionally, so they dropped us off half a mile short. The final stretch of that road was a lunar surface with shoulder-to-shoulder potholes. Today it's the heavily traveled main access to gigantic Bell Labs.

On safaris into the great unknown one had to plan as best he could, after long consultations with earlier explorers and diligent comparisons of alternate routes with their varying hazards, and then take a leap of faith. On one such probe four of us youngsters took off from northern New Jersey for as far south as we could get during spring vacation of a high-school year, ultimately penetrating coastal North Carolina. Nobody we knew had ever been 'way down there and returned to tell the tale. We had to venture to the rim of the known world—roughly Washington, D.C.—and after that plunge into the abyss. It proved to be a fine trip, highly educational, marred by no incident, and blessed with perfect weather. We spent our nights in groves of stately trees or barns or fairgrounds—motels, even of the mom-and-pop variety, were still in the future—and met unfailingly gracious people, happy to cooperate and pass the time of day. We told them tales, they told us better tales. They spoke an odd, soft, liquid language, they had strange tastes in food, they were apt to be fishing in the dark waters of slow-flowing streams when they could have been painting an outhouse, they seemed in no hurry to get life over with, they were fine folk. Even the chain gangs were relaxed and happy.

I didn't know then that, five hundred miles westward, North Carolina soared heavenward in the mighty upthrust of the Southern Appalachians, with Mount Mitchell brooding over all and the French Broad River somehow snaking its way through them on its journey to the Mississippi. I could not know then that there, in and around Asheville, I was to find my permanent home here below, and in that land, among its people, I would learn to like grits, okra, and black-eyed peas and spend the best part of my mature life.

When the appointed time came, I would love that high country at first sight, possibly because it so resembled New England. In my youth I continued to fancy that God created New England first, in the prime of a full vigor, lavishing upon it His best ideas. All the rest of the world was spillover. I am just as provincial in another way now that I know western North Carolina. However, you stay where you are. You're happy there, or at least adjusted to your fate.

But North Carolina's mountains are not visible from her Outer Banks, by which I mean that you cannot see far ahead when you are on a trip, and it's foolish to try. We do live by faith, not by sight. Of course, it's wise to glance forward, from time to time, to where the road bends and cuts off the long view, but mostly you had best look around where you are and savor the present moment. I really do know, love, honor, and frequently obey that truth, yet nowadays I travel by interstate, following a detailed map, skimming the surface, getting there but seeing nobody and nothing en route.

Nothing was what you were apt to see if you had to travel by night back in the days of my youth. The electrical system of aging Model T's was subject to a senile debility whereby you had a choice of lights or locomotion, but not both at once. Naturally you opted for motion, trusting that any oncoming wayfarer wasn't in your identical fix or that maybe the moon would rise. At forks in the road you stopped, if haply there was a signpost, revved up the engine to full throttle, switched on the lights, and got your bearings by their momentary glow. After your eyes reacquired night vision, you groped onward in darkness, perhaps meditating on the human predicament in general.

Doubtless we experienced no mechanical trouble on the afore-mentioned trip because we made it in a brand-new car available to an affluent friend. It had probably cost his father nearly four hundred dollars. My own automobiles never cost more than twenty-five dollars until I was through college, was steadily employed, and married. Obviously these bargain-basement specials were not in mint condition. Early cars were rugged, employed a minimum of parts, and indulged in no gee-gaws at all, but a hundred thousand miles would take some of the bloom off them.

In self-defense I became a passable backyard mechanic, like the rest of my generation. The labyrinthian innards of a modern auto-mobile terrify me into a prudent hands-off policy, but back then any fool could keep a Tin Lizzie running, and we all did. Henry Ford had contrived a simple functional machine, with nothing esoteric between its straightforward motor and its rear wheels. Besides, his invention had a mind of its own and frequently fixed itself, after a bout of the sulks. An activist might fancy he had done something creative by rapping the commutator with a wrench, but in truth he had only vented his frustrations. Model T would have brought itself around by morning, chances are. Nevertheless we all knew how to grind valves, renew brakebands, replace differentials, and above all repair tires. The fellow who thought up the demountable rim should be enshrined in a Hall of Fame. I am especially glad he had his epochal thought before the day when four of us Amherst undergraduates set out to watch our football team play against and at Princeton. On that simple little jaunt we had to repair eleven flat tires, which we considered to be about par for the course in a twenty-dollar jalopy. Come to think of it, we had to replace a burned-out bearing, too—Model T's finicky number-one bearing. We all knew that on really long hills we should turn the car around and back up the grade for a while to make sure that some oil nourished number-one, but we gambled, and of course we lost. So did Amherst, also of course.

In those casual days vehicle safety took a back seat to vehicle function. On an occasion when the steering column of my then-flivver came away from the dashboard, I kept driving it homeward with the steering wheel in my lap, until the sheer awkwardness of the situation suggested roadside first-aid. I simply wired the column back approximately whence it came, drove home, and left this loaded weapon in our driveway while I rummaged in the shed for permanent repair material. Mother chose this moment for a trip downtown, perforce using my car, which blocked hers.

As everybody should know, the gas lever of a Model T erupted to the right of the steering wheel, and in the case of mine now moved with the whole column. Naturally when Mother made a left turn out of our driveway the car slowed to a bucking crawl. This puzzled her, but she made some adjustments and kept on going townward.

Under the best of circumstances Mother's driving commanded respect; lots of people darted into a side street or at least pulled to the curb when they saw her coming. Her weavings and tackings on this trip were undoubtedly more sweeping than usual, but I imagine nobody thought much of it. They just gave her the customary clear field, so there was no manslaughter when she made a right turn in the center of town and the car shot forward like a scared rabbit, straight up the steps of the First National Bank. It stalled there among the Corinthian columns.

You had to drive my contraption with a finger hooked around the gas lever to compensate for turns, but this adaptation had not occurred to Mother. She wasn't mechanically inclined. When the bank teller brought her home, she wasn't even interested in my scientific explanations. She preferred to think my car was hexed. The teller preferred that I retrieve it, at once. I went back with him and did so, to the cheers of the citizenry. The cop on the beat gave me interested assistance, but nothing more. He had known Mother for years. I thanked him, drove the car home, and unhexed it. Mother, when so notified, said she didn't believe in exorcism and wouldn't touch that thing again with a ten-foot pole.

Model T rather dominates this account, I realize, but that's proper because it did exactly that during the whole era. Not too many of us ordinary mortals went in much for Duesenbergs, Cadillacs, or Cords. The finest classic car we were likely to own would be the Ford Model A, the Baby Lincoln, with its lovely pure lines and another of Henry's no-nonsense, foolproof mechanisms. Mine was one of his blue convertible roadsters with a rumble seat. I drove it during many happy years, and I think I wish I could get another one in these last days, when the automobile is trying to come full circle. Occasionally I do still see a Model A on the highway, and my heart leaps. Maybe I used to own that very one.

I did briefly enjoy a new Chrysler Imperial for a while in 1930. The exact date is easy to remember because a friend lent it to my wife and me for our wedding trip, the start of which was considerably delayed. The bride-to-be was heading for the church on a shortcut back road without houses or traffic when her family's old Willys Knight conked out. It wouldn't restart, and nothing passed by except the scheduled hour of the wedding. She began wondering if the faithful old Willys was trying to tell her something; it had never failed before. There was some consternation at the church, too. Watches were being consulted, eyebrows elevated, questioning glances shared. The collective blood pressure was pretty high when the bridal party finally showed up, rescued by a passing Overland. I thought my clergyman grandfather took pains to tie a good strong knot, which has in fact lasted us a lifetime.

An hour or so into our honeymoon trip toward Painted Post, New York, where I was to resume working for Ingersoll-Rand, we both began to relax, soothed by that purring Imperial. "I didn't know that cars like this existed," my bride said. She added, as wives will, "Could we afford to buy one?"

"We'll get two of them," I told her, as grooms will. Besides, all things seemed possible back in those years when all the world was young. "We'll get one for you and one for me."

We didn't. We got that Model A, which fitted nicely into a basement garage, and lived happily ever after.

Thus we began life's adventure, heading eagerly northward on the course we ourselves, in our less than infinite wisdom, had charted. In the really Infinite Wisdom we ended up in a precisely opposite direction, as you already know. Sometimes we all do wonder what our lives would have been like if we had insisted upon taking a different turning point at any of a thousand crossroads. I admit to curiosity on the subject, but I am content that on our developing journey we had the, at times, reluctant grace to follow the route deemed best by our all-wise Travel Agent. The scenery along the road we actually traveled could not possibly be excelled, nor could the people in whose company we made the trip or the souvenirs we collected along the way.

And now, after a long and circuitous journey, we have at last returned to that North Carolina boarding school which we left on hold several chapters back in order to go on a search for roots. From here on the course is straight forward.

SEVEN

Oak Ridge

Bless me, Father, if I have sinned.

I seem to recall that there was a long period in the history of the Church when clergy were forbidden to engage themselves in secular work. If so, and if the inhibition is still on the books, manifestly I have (without any sense of guilt) grievously disobeyed the rules of the order. Bless me, Father, if I have sinned. I confess that I drove a huge Euclid one whole summer, moving monstrous amounts of dirt to make some needed money and, incidentally, an airplane runway. During several football seasons throughout the years of my school chaplaincy I regularly officiated, for hire, at night games between the local high schools. (Driving home quite late from one of these we suffered a flat tire and discovered that we had no jack. After several passersby actually speeded up when I hailed them, it finally dawned on us to hide me in the woods while my wife flagged down a rescuer. The poor fellow experienced severe trauma when, brandishing a lug wrench, I stepped forth arrayed in the black-and-white stripes of an escaped convict.) And throughout forty years, somewhat hidden behind a pen name, I wrote stories, articles, essays, and books on a variety of very mundane matters, for very mundane reasons. Worst of all, I helped build Oak Ridge.

The duties of a school chaplain aren't all that confining in the long vacation (the same is not true of a headmaster), so for a couple of summers during World War Two I was free to labor at the Manhattan Project over in Tennessee, returning to North Carolina on weekends to take Sunday services. Those weekly round trips by automobile required considerable gasoline, which the Ration Board immediately granted. I needed four new tires too and was allotted them at once. So, although there were a dozen theories but no firm knowledge about what we were doing at Oak Ridge, the evidence was clear that it was top priority. When you said "Manhattan Project," you got action from the Board, and you got it right now. It was awesome, in the days when there was little gas and less rubber, to watch frozen colonels with "No" written all over their faces come to attention, thaw, smile, and approve your application before you even began offering your prepared argument.

As to what we were doing: The firm I was with had the contract for roofing and sheet-metal work on the vast complex at K-25. My ultimate work as chief timekeeper and paymaster took me out of the office for a couple of hours each day to check up on the men, and during one such absence the rest of our office staff heard a fifteen-minute radio broadcast from Knoxville purporting to describe exactly what Oak Ridge was all about. They were discussing it when I returned and arrived at the consensus that the report made sense, or at least fitted in with what we had all noticed. That broadcast was never repeated. It was never denied. It was never referred to again. It simply became a nonevent, à la 1984. After the war, when the accuracy of the broadcast was substantiated, it became obvious that heads had rolled because of that leak. Perhaps General Groves had personally boiled the commentator in oil. Perhaps, for lack of time in the press of his duties, he had had to delegate the privilege to deserving subordinates.

Meanwhile K-25 kept on rising, just as the pyramids of Egypt had in their day. So many men swarmed over the project that daily progress simply had to happen. My own firm had a fixed-price contract, and our men put out, steadily and hard. Our office cynics claimed that all other contractors were on cost-plus, hence their laborers dawdled. I wouldn't know. I do know that Murphy's Law prevailed at Oak Ridge, and with good reason.

Because of the pressure of time—would the Germans beat us to IT?—the vast Manhattan Project erupted straight out of a test tube, without any intervening pilot plant. Multitudinous change-orders were, therefore, inevitable. Sometimes it seemed that what was built today had to be torn down tomorrow to make room for a fresh start in a new direction.

Furthermore there was a war on, and skilled labor was in short supply. Many of our workers had been recruited from the agricultural areas of the Deep South, induced to come aboard by draft deferment and big pay—an incredible $1.10 per hour. Their industrial experience was nil, and in some cases their IQs not much more. We did have experienced artisans fabricating the sections of sheet-metal ducts that were to run for miles through the enormous buildings, but within a week it fell to my lot to show the erectors how those sections went together. You know as much about sheet-metal work as I do, provided you are totally ignorant on the subject, but I had once worked for Ingersoll-Rand, was somewhat literate, and above all could decipher a blueprint. So I showed those erectors what to do and how to do it. It's my understanding that the ventilating ducts—if that's what they were—are still in place and possibly still functional.

Before getting any deeper into this, let it be clear that I was indeed an authorized sheet-metal man and had a union card to prove it. This innocent and incognito and ignorant clergyman had walked into a ten-by-twelve shed housing a desk and chair upon which sat a beefy man in a derby hat, chewing a dead cigar just like in a B-movie. The preacher forked over fifteen dollars, signed here, and walked out the door a transmigrated soul, a validated sheet-metal man with a testimonial proving it. Many of my coworkers, who had undergone the same indoctrination course, were fully as skilled as I.

All of this know-how was often aborted because communication between the various contractors left much to be desired. Our fabricators, all of them genuine sheet-metal men, worked in one huge room making sections of duct. Our erectors, many of them ex-cotton-pickers, put these parts together and into place far across the way, working with the segments that their adept blueprint-reader and his crew lugged over to place in proper order before them. Well and good, except when we reported for work in the morning and found that night-shift carpenters had put up a catwalk for electricians to work on high overhead. Usually the supports and cross-braces of that catwalk blocked the entrance to our duct gallery. A starved hound-dog might have squeezed between them, but not a couple of hefty Alabama field hands carting a ten-foot segment of ductwork three feet in cross-section. Electricians and sheet-metal men stood around while day-shift carpenters tore down the night work and put it back up again, this time with the supports in the obviously sensible places.

Union rules came into play, too. A crew of five electricians, in hanging a series of transformers, would be using a wooden ladder which was lightly spiked to that scaffold lest it slip. The work having been finished at one location and the ensuing cigarette-break consummated, one electrician ultimately wandered off in search of a pair of carpenters competent and authorized to draw a spike, move a ladder to its next appointed spot, tap the spike back in again, and return to their own abandoned project. Act Two, a carbon copy of Act One, would then be played out by the electricians.

Absenteeism, of which Oak Ridge had its share, always sabotages efficiency. I imagine it prevails on every construction site. Men living far from home in hot barracks, facing a boring weekend with unaccustomed big money burning their pockets, surely are occasionally tempted to go out on the town. In fact, they have been known to include Friday in the spree, and to stretch it through Monday by choice or necessity. Working on Monday with bleary eyes and a broken head is not attractive. It is completely inhibited when you've ended up in jail.

My work as timekeeper and paymaster, whereby I came to know the men better than anybody else in our office, naturally moved me over into personnel. In this unofficial capacity I frequently met The Law, from deputy sheriff up to and including the FBI. Let's say that Willie turned up missing for too many days, throwing his whole roofing crew out of gear. Along about Wednesday I'd hunt him down, from barracks to infirmary to jail.

"Why didn't you telephone us?" I'd ask poor repentant Willie through his bars.

"I as't to," Willie would mumble. "Dey jes' laft, an' tole me tuh use duh phone in duh cohnah of mah cell."

It's been my experience that few jail cells have private telephones. Willie's certainly didn't. But the sheriff would be glad to get rid of him, now that a responsible person could vouch for his future. First there had to be conversation, of course. I'd hold a lengthy heart-to-heart one with Willie, then report back to the sheriff.

"Willie's all right," I'd assure him. "We've known him a long time. Good man, good worker, with a good record back home in Asheville. We know his whole family there. Good people. Well, Willie made a mistake, but he's broke now, and in the future I'll be sending most of his pay straight home for him. He's just told me that's what he wants, and that's what I'll do. He won't be giving you any trouble again."

"Mebbe." A doodle, while the mental wheels went 'round. "But those stupid Feds think he's dangerous. They found this on him." He'd show me a short, sharp, wicked-looking, hawk-billed throat-cutter.

"Willie's a roofer," I'd explain. "You know as well as I do that that's a roofer's tool, for cutting felt."

69

We'd get Willie back, his crew would come to life, and the job would go forward. But next week another key man would turn up missing.

It's hard to blame them. A roofer works up there under the blazing Tennessee sun, in the midst of hot tar. At the end of the day he descends into choking dust or knee-deep mire. Few diversions await him—perhaps poker or arguing or fighting, or all three in that order. His food is not gourmet. "Don't eat the blueberry pie," the cafeteria loudspeakers would rasp. "It could poison you." I had dysentery for days and nights on end the second summer I worked over there. It's a most unpleasant affliction. You lose, among other things, your zip. One afternoon I simply had to crawl inside a ventilator and sleep the hours away. I wasn't missed, the work continued without my personal assistance, and the Manhattan Project finally got built.

Our little barracks-fellowship was playing bridge the night the loudspeakers screamed the news about Hiroshima. Immediately there was portent, an ominous restlessness, in the air. Our game palled. We let the cards lie and fell to speculating about the atomic bomb, pooling our ignorances to keep the conversation going.

When morning dawned, we learned that a lot of construction workers had vanished during the night. Those who remained explained that their departed cohorts were afraid the whole place could blow up in their faces at any moment. At first I honored those frightened escapees more than I did the others who left in a body a week later, after Japan surrendered. It seemed to me these were openly admitting that draft dodging had been the prime force that kept them working.

With time my judgment mellowed. I began to think that maybe they just wanted to go home, now that the job was done. For despite everything, the job had indeed been done, never to be undone. They gave us all an Army-Navy E, for Excellence, to prove it; to certify that we had had a hand in making stardust, whereby the whole place could indeed blow up in our faces at any moment.

IN TOUCH

EIGHT

Potholes and Preaching

*Only two of them—my wife and the Senior Warden—
realized that something unusual was afoot.*

Frank, normally a most punctual fellow, was an hour late for our
appointment. My wristwatch gave me this objective information,
but the timepiece of impatience made him much tardier than that.
In a way it told the deeper truth; Frank was more than half a year
behind time. Some eight months ago we had decided to go prospect-
ing for gold here in our North Carolina mountains at the first
mutually available opportunity. This was the scheduled day, at long
last, and still Frank hadn't shown.

I found it impossible to put real dedication into the chores I
invented to fill out the time. They all needed to be done; they all
had been laid on the shelf for precisely such an interval as this; but
impatience is a hard driver, especially impatience for gold. I began
to understand gold fever as I patched a hole in the window screen, as
I cleaned and oiled the power mower, as I tidied up the garage.

Frank was as frustrated as I was and full of apologies when his Jeep finally lurched into my driveway. He had awakened with a stabbing toothache, the kind you can't put off, so he had wheedled a dentist friend into treating him at eight o'clock. It was either that or telephone me and call our whole plan off again. I sympathized, piled my gear in with his, jumped aboard, and we were off at last.

The old abandoned mine, which had yielded a few million dollars' worth of gold in a high state of purity, is an hour distant from our town—through valleys, across creeks, into the hills, and up ancient logging roads in the back of beyond where only four-wheel drive can go, and sometimes you wonder about that. You wonder also about the breed of men who found this treasure and others like it in the first place, without benefit of Jeeps. Our whole surrounding area is dotted with worked-out mines of one sort or another, most of them all but inaccessible even today. Twice that morning Frank, busy with his plunging Jeep, pointed with his head at deep forested draws and shouted, "Know about that old corundum mine down there?" While I memorized some bearing points for future reference, I marveled at our rugged forebears who disappeared into this wilderness on foot or muleback and somehow found these impossible places. There were giants in the earth in those days.

Of course they had a different sense of time from ours, and they probably didn't pack their days so full of many things as we do now. When they went after gold or precious stones, they headed straight for their chosen Grail, stripped down for the job. Frank and I, modern civilized fellows with a lot of pressing affairs on our minds—Frank is involved with power dams all over the country—understandably had to wait half a year for this outing.

Frank finally braked to a stop where the trail crossed a creek. "The old mine's about fifty yards above us, on the right," he said. "This would be as good a place as any to start panning." Our theory was that if there still was a trace of gold in these hills, as there once had been in vast quantity, the creek below the mine was its logical location. We chose our places and started panning.

Panning wasn't difficult or tiring—a brief lesson gives anybody the knack—but digging for material was rough. My feeling was that any gold, which is heavy, would be down at the bottom of things, deep within the sandy silt piled up behind rocks and fallen trees. So I didn't fool much with the surface of things; I dug deep and panned the bottom stuff. I worked eagerly and hard, so that after a couple of hours some long-neglected muscles in my shoulders began giving me the word.

Soon I was taking time out at frequent intervals, sitting on a mossy boulder easing my aches and savoring a pipe while idly watching the dappled shadows and the occasional birds. Frank had completely disappeared from sight and sound. I was alone, but far from lonely. From time to time I went back into action—after all, this was what we thought we had come for—perhaps working a couple of hours more in all. The unaccustomed body can stand just so much, however, and unrewarded enthusiasm does run down in the fiercest blood. Besides, the enormous spell of the forest was running competition to the lure of gold. Flowing brook and noonday stillness were hypnotic. Once I found myself merely sitting at the base of a gigantic poplar—it must have been eighteen feet around—just looking at everything and nothing. I couldn't remember how long, or how briefly, I had been sitting there caught up in nature's parables.

As the day wore higher, Frank and I gravitated back toward one another to pan, without zest, on opposite sides of the same small pool. Before too long Frank lit a cigarette and quit with clear finality, an example I was happy to imitate. We sat there in silence, watching the ripples run over the smooth stones. After the water cleared, we took a long cold drink and struggled back to the Jeep, empty-handed.

Since there was a lot of day left and our curious lust for gold was completely gone, we drove on down to the river a few miles below us to eat our belated lunch. The trail continued in that direction, overgrown but good enough for the laboring Jeep, and Frank remembered a spectacular picnic site.

I believed him with good reason because we were in spectacular country. It is built on an awe-inspiring scale, without there being— to my emotions—anything threatening about it. I do realize that it gives some flatlanders psychological trouble. Often I have seen them cringe back, in primitive terror, from the heights we have around here. To drive our tortuous highways in the summer is, quite often, to creep along behind a paralyzed Floridian who is fearfully inching around the mountain, as far from the guard rail as possible.

Once I came upon a Miami Beach-type mincing her way down the macadam in her party shoes, with her mink stole flapping in the breeze. "My friend's driving our car, up there around the bend," she wailed through her tears. "I have to walk ahead to warn you she's on the wrong side of the road. We can't *possibly* drive out *there!*" A wave of the hand toward outer space, followed by a dreadful shudder. "Please, when you pass her, *you* use the outside lane."

I don't know why some of us are mountain people, free and easy and at home in the enfolding hills, while others become depressed or even fearful there. Or why I, for my part, am bored and somewhat lost on the great flat plains where other people's spirits soar and where they exultingly cry, "Look how far you can see!" ("See what?" I always want to ask.) It may be that they are the really adjusted people, or at least the outgoing kind. It may be that we mountaineers are insecure, or withdrawn, so that we need to be palpably inside our snug walls. However that may be, Frank and I careened quite casually down the impossible trail through the huge benign hills, rolling relaxed inside the pitching vehicle.

Frank was right about picnicking by the river—a river those Miami ladies will never see. Swelled by hundreds of tributary streams like our gold-panning creek, that powerful torrent rushes through a deep rocky gorge in the heart of the mountains, now foaming across boulders big as houses and around great slabs of granite upended every which way, now sliding clear and almost oily across wide flats. On this gorgeous day, with towering green hemlocks etched against an incredible blue sky, it flowed in technicolor on the level and crashed milky-white down the cataracts.

76

Out in the clear pools by the rocks we could see ten feet and more to the sandy white bottom, dappled with the shadows of ripples and the substance of trout swimming idly in and out of hiding.

We lingered on the rocks above it, listening to its muffled roar and inspecting the potholes cut into the granite by the action of water during the centuries. Some of those holes were high and dry—far above the present water level in spite of the fact that the river was in spate now after several days of heavy rain. It gave you some idea of how long that water had been rushing down the gorge, working patiently, smoothly wearing down the rock and settling ever deeper into its bed. How many millennia ago was it when those upper potholes, now full of dry leaves and twigs, were under water? How long does it take a river to cut a pothole several feet across and perhaps eight feet deep into granite—starting with some tiny fault in the rock where a few grains of sand could lodge and the water could begin swirling them around, grinding imperceptibly while the centuries passed?

We climbed down finally, washed in one of the huge round bathtubs whose sides were slick as glass, and ate our lunch on a table of rock jutting over the stream. The trout proved avid for crusts of bread and crumbs of hard-cooked egg yolk. After eating we lounged on our rock in the warm afternoon sun, not talking much, just thoroughly content to be there. The day was almost gone before a quick dip in the cold river jolted us back into life.

After we had dried and dressed, we climbed slowly back up to the trail and took one last look at the river roaring along beneath us, as it had been doing for millions of years now and as it would continue to do for millions of years to come. "Some people might call that a lot of wasted energy," I said.

Frank, the water-power man, studied the river for a while. Then his gaze lingered on the granite cliffs, the hemlocks, the encircling mountains, and finally the clear sky. A vapor trail against the infinite blue told us that a jet plane was passing high above us, making its exclamation point in the heavens. The plane itself was no more visible to us than we two specks were to it. We were all tucked away in our various immensities.

"Those same people might think that you and I wasted our energy today," Frank said finally. "Which reminds me." He fumbled in his pocket, found what he was looking for, passed it over to me, and watched me while I studied it.

"Yeah, it's pure gold," he said when I handed it back, looking my question at him. "The dentist took it out of my tooth this morning. I beat it into nugget shape to salt your pan with when you weren't looking. Somehow I forgot to do that." He twirled the gold a while between his thumb and finger, then tossed the nugget in a long high arc into the river. "I'm glad I forgot," he went on. "Gold would have ruined the day. Let the trout have it."

We stood there a few more minutes, until the vapor trail above us began to disintegrate and fade away. "Let me know when you're going to preach a sermon that has its root in this day," Frank said. "I just might come to hear it." He climbed into the Jeep. "Right now we'd best get started. We've got a long tough trip ahead of us before we get back home."

As Frank indicated, sermons often arise from, have their roots in, the interplay of the natural with the supernatural. The Divine Alchemist easily makes gold out of lead. So it may well be that I ultimately drew half a dozen spiritual talks from the total experience of that uneventful day which, upon reflection, I came to see was a parable of the entire story of our development along the Purgative and Illuminative Ways toward the Unitive State. To those with ears to hear, like Frank, it spoke loud and clear of the Mystic Way.

I don't know that Frank came to hear my efforts, however, or indeed that he needed to, and thus is outlined the scope of this essay. It is not concerned with the benefits, if any, that sermons may bring to their hearers. It confines itself to the contributions sermons bring to the preacher himself, to their part in the shaping of a priest.

As a matter of fact I would be among the last people on earth to make great claims for the value of sermons in the spiritual regime of their intended victims. The skepticism may stem from a traumatic experience of mine, although I don't really think that it does. In any case, I was holding forth from the pulpit one Sunday, in fine fettle, when *in medias res* I was stricken with excruciating physical pain which brought a cold sweat to my brow and a weakness just short of fainting to my whole body. I hesitate to ascribe the cause to the sermon itself; no sermon could possibly be that bad. It is more probable that a kidney stone was acting up. Whatever the cause I simply could not continue preaching. In fact, I could hardly stagger out of the pulpit, cross the chancel, and collapse in the sacristy.

Before thus departing, however, I stammered to the congregation in halting words that my projected address was perforce unfinished, but doubtless they could readily complete my thoughts by themselves. The congregation numbered about five hundred. Only two of them—my wife and the Senior Warden—realized that something unusual was afoot. These came swiftly to the sacristy with aid and comfort. Four hundred and ninety-eight souls, however, apparently were not so much as aware that my little weekly gem lacked its usual symmetry and final polish.

Even without this graphic commentary on the eternal importance of sermons in the saving of other souls than my own, I would be a poor judge of the matter. During my active years I heard few sermons—perhaps one or two a year, as when the Bishop came—because most of the time I had no associate clergy with whom to share the privilege. (When one does have several curates, he can point to one of them five minutes before the service begins and say, "You preach today." I have heard that this occurs, and that the practice helps keep junior brethren on their toes. Once, even when the Bishop came, something similar happened to me. Ten minutes before service time I was saying to him, "Just before the sermon the master of ceremonies will come to lead you to the pulpit—" when he interrupted to say, "I'm not preaching today. You are." Of course I did so, being a man under obedience and utterly helpless besides. If you must know, I preached extemporaneously on the first three Stations of the Cross: Jesus is condemned to death; Jesus receives the cross; Jesus falls under the weight of the cross. The topic seemed à propos.)

On vacations I would attend the then-sermonless early Celebration so that I could compete in an archery tournament later in the day. Now in my latter days I hear few if any pulpit talks because of my deafness. That's all right because I usually do manage to catch the text, upon which I can expatiate to myself, it is to be hoped with the aid of the Holy Spirit.

Sermons do the active cleric enormous good, however, because they compel him to diligence. Of course a preacher must be continually studying, must make an annual Retreat, must maintain a disciplined spiritual life in its entire range, or his well will ultimately run dry. Beyond that, he must acquire the habit of going about all his days attentively looking and listening for what God is saying to him in the events or boredoms of those days. He must live in two worlds at once, so passing through things temporal that he loses not the things eternal. He must also be continually moving about alertly and lovingly among his parishioners, absorbing what God is saying to him through them. In the process he will thus learn from them what is in their hearts and on their minds, and so be saved from preaching in a vacuum, from answering questions that have not been raised, from casting seed on unplowed ground. Naturally when he pulls together all this ammunition into a sermon and shoots it forth in the general direction of his audience, he must aim slightly over his own and their heads, without in any degree talking down. Yet he must remain in touch, not over the hill out of sight.

There are certain little warning indications that a sermon is not getting across because it is on the wrong wavelength. The audience is a captive one, well-bred, courteous, and willing to remain courteous to the bitter end. They will seldom wind their watches during a sermon, however tedious it may be. Even more rarely will they shake them to make sure they haven't run down. Almost never will they in final puzzlement hold them to their ears to determine whether they are functioning. Yet all of us seasoned preachers can detect an elusive apathetic restlessness in the congregation that reveals lack of contact. The women are mentally rearranging their living room furniture. The men are reading the bulletin for the third time. This is not a good occasion for the preacher to shout and brandish his arms; the damage has irretrievably been done. It is the proper time to say "finally" and finish.

Given the above-mentioned "remote" preparation for preaching, each week brings the labor of "proximate" preparation. The preacher has to select a topic from the available legion. He has to meditate upon and about it in his prayer life, thereby giving God an opportunity to get a word in, to lead him into truths that lie under the surface. He has to winnow and order his thoughts on the subject, giving his exposition of it a recognizable, not to say arresting, beginning, middle, and end. (Sermons really should end, not more than twelve minutes after they begin.) He has to find the proper words in which to express his, and occasionally God's, mind on the matter. He has to set these proper words edge to edge in their correct order. He must select, preferably from his own but in a pinch somebody else's treasury, illustrations that deftly illuminate and clarify his subject.

The process is plain hard work, most of the time, but often is worth it, for it can lead the preacher far more deeply into eternal truth than he realized on Tuesday morning when he began the venture. Thus, sermon preparation does him a lot of good, long before he steps into the pulpit.

Once there, even while on his way there, he must try to hold firmly in mind that his delicately fashioned jewel is not a finished and immortal work of art, not an end in itself, but rather is a means to an end. It is a tool. It must *do* something—intrigue, instruct, convince, console, convict, even if possible convert his hearers. An old chestnut comes to mind: a candidate for Holy Orders timidly hands his Bishop a manuscript of the canonically required sermon, and asks, "Bishop, will this do?" To which the Bishop replies, "Do what?" The problem is not solved by preaching "lettuce" sermons, by the way; sermons in which the peroration consists of "let us" be up and doing.

In the pulpit the preacher, if he is to profit, must remember to forget himself, to ignore the dulcet and beguiling sound of his own voice, to be unknowing or at least indifferent as to whether his better profile is in the spotlight, and to eschew pulpit-pounding. He said he was speaking in the Name of the Father and of the Son and of the Holy Ghost. He must really mean it. They speak in a still small voice. They persuade, rather than bludgeon, because the more spiritual a matter is, the farther removed it is from the realm of coercive power. Perhaps the best way to do all this is to think of sermonizing as talking to oneself out loud. If others care to listen in, they may, at their own risk.

If and when he does these things in these ways, the sermon will be a good one. A very good one. Should the congregation, in filing out after the service, say not a word to him about it but go their quiet ways homeward, chances are it was an excellent sermon. If so, in order to squeeze the last bit of good out of it, he must forget all about that sermon and begin turning his mind toward the next one.

Yet he cannot wholly forget, for in spite of all his self-effacement he has experienced valid satisfaction in a job done for the glory of God to the very best of his present ability. So a few years later, when he has been called to fields of wider service where he is so desperately busy that he has no time to think yet must speedily find something to say and a way to say it because Sunday is breathing down his neck, he hunts down that old but well-remembered sermon to see if haply he might preach it again, perhaps using different illustrations. He finds it among his other treasures, he begins to read it, and he has to pinch his nostrils. A stale stench is rising from his whole precious barrel of sermons. He shudders and throws his masterpiece away, realizing how dreadful it is. Nevertheless it was still an excellent sermon in its time. Partly because of it, he has grown above it.

I cannot tell you what he did preach about that Sunday, for I have forgotten what it was, but preach he did, for Sunday inexorably rolls around. The best I can say is that he preached about twelve minutes.

This is probably a good place to say that one of my reasons for hesitating about entering the ministry was that I was terrified at the thought of having to attend a Sunday School picnic every year and preach a sermon every week. In the actual event this proved to be merely groundless fear of the unknown. Sunday School picnics were a lot of fun.

NINE

Early Archery

. . . you took away the excess and freed the
captive creature hidden there.

By "early" archery I don't mean a speculation on how the unsung
genius who invented the bow managed to arrive at his elliptical
conclusion. Nor do I have in mind the utterly fascinating history of
this ancient and honorable instrument of sport and warfare, this
storied vehicle of romance and poetry. I am referring only to the
beginning stages of the astonishing renaissance of American archery in our time.

To get a running start we can remind ourselves that the use of
bow and arrow in this country was all but abandoned by, say, 1850.
Even our Indians quit using it, turning to powder and ball. Immediately after the Civil War, Maurice and Will Thompson did pick up
the fallen weapon and put it to extraordinary use. One of these
brothers had suffered a chest injury and had been condemned by his
doctor to live an outdoor life—I regret that I do not have the

doctor's name and address. In the 1870s the Thompsons began to publish stories of their hunting with the bow, and soon their classic book *The Witchery of Archery* made its appearance.

Yet this was, as it turned out, a false dawn. Archery yielded to lawn tennis, bicycle riding, and bloomers. The sun set on the sport for nearly forty years. So far as I know, only the United Bowmen of Philadelphia, an austere and exclusive club founded in 1818, maintained activity during the Tunnel Period. But its membership was limited to fifty in number, and lesser men could tread the sacred sod of the United Bowmen's hallowed range only upon special invitation.

Archery began its really modern revival about 1920. Saxton Pope and Arthur Young are the great bow-hunting names of those early years; Howard Hill would come along a bit later. If one fixed date for the birth of modern archery is desired, 1924 will serve as well as any. In that year Dr. Pope published his *Hunting with the Bow.*

That makes me a son of the pioneers, for I took up archery around 1935 under most fortunate circumstances—I had state and national champions, like Dutch Weese and Ree Dillinger, as cohorts, and although the mighty revival had strongly begun, we were still in the classical period. Bows continued to be made of wood, on the English longbow model. There was lemonwood, that satisfactory and obedient material. Even I, equipped with my ten thumbs, could make a decent bow of lemonwood at the expense of a couple of dollars and a little time. I could buy a better one for five dollars. My first bow was lemonwood, and I still have half a dozen of them down in the cellar despite the score or so I have given away in seducing others to take up this aspect of romance. The beginner did well to launch out with lemonwood.

Then there was Osage orange, far tougher, more enduring, more deadly. You couldn't mass-produce good Osage bows—and surely a faint protest against the machine age is involved in archery's modern resurrection. Each Osage bow was an individual, painstakingly constructed with drawknife and sandpaper according to the knots and twists and peculiar grain structure of the billet that came your way. You worked on them with the care God lavishes on human souls. Osage made lovely bows, strong, stout, solid bows. They had character, dependability, perseverance, fortitude. You could get careless with them—bump them against a fence post or a tree or a boulder accidentally—and they would forgive you. One of my early hunting bows was made of Osage. It was a beautifully ugly, gnarled specimen full of checks and dutchmen—these are technical terms, without reference to nationality—but it shot wonderfully well, and I couldn't hurt it.

And then there was that queen of bow woods, the truly magnificent yew, imported from Spain or grown in our own state of Oregon. You spent eight or ten dollars for a three-foot billet of yew that had been cut, six or eight years before, on the north slope of a snowclad mountain in the sapless wintertime. You called in your mad cronies to study and discuss the grain of this expensive piece of firewood with you. Then, while everybody held his breath, you split the log like a diamond.

The next step was to saw out a V- or W-joint in the ends of your billets and glue them together end to end, so that the upper and lower limbs of your projected bow would work together in the sweet harmony of twins who had slumbered side by side for decades in the womb of their mother tree. And then you carved, or sculpted, your bow from this result, night after night in the quiet cellar. Not doing what you felt like doing, not imposing your will upon nature, but following the contours and the grain that nature had laid down. You took away the excess and freed the captive creature hidden there. Carving thus creatively on wood, especially such a uniquely responsive and rewarding wood as yew, can be an authentic religious experience for the two or three gathered together around the workbench, or altar. The coffee and sandwiches served afterwards, savored in the midst of incense rising from sawdust and shavings, are remotely akin to Midnight Mass and Holy Communion.

The sweetest bow I ever owned was made of yew. It was lovely to look at, with its deep orange heartwood and its ivory sapwood marked off in clean lines, and with its grain never running out. It was light in the hand, as yew always is. It drew smoothly, building up steadily and evenly, with no sudden jumps or dead spots. And it shot with authority, with flat trajectory, without kick or twist. It was alive.

Indeed, I assisted at its birth. I was watching over the shoulder of a friend, one of the great bowyers of our or any time who had kindly come to be with me on the final night, when it became a living thing. One moment it was just a stick of wood. Then my friend passed the knife over it another time, and it was a vibrant, dynamic, living entity.

Fifty years ago everybody felt about his bow as I felt about that one—which I still have, you may be sure. Bows were completely personal. Each was one-of-a-kind, an individual masterpiece. You knew yours as a friend, his weak points and his strong ones, his character and his quirks. You could insult a man by insulting his bow. Greater love had no man than this—that he would offer you the use of his bow. Of course no real archer would accept the offer.

Yet I unwittingly witnessed an even greater act of love than that during the afternoon, the second half, of a major tournament. I was in the thick of things on Target One when my bowstring broke. I rummaged through my tackle box for a spare string, but to my consternation none was there. It developed later that my children had borrowed them and neglected to put them back, but that is another story. At the moment I was thunderstruck.

Davey, a friend and parishioner, noticed my misfortune from where he was doing very well down on Target Three. He swiftly brought me a string, which fitted my own bow nicely. With only a couple of tightening twists it more than adequately replaced my useless one, and I continued shooting.

Only later, much later, did I learn that Davey didn't continue shooting. He couldn't. He had taken the string off his own bow to give to me and had dropped out of the tournament.

All too soon wooden bows became things of the past. Up and down the tournament lines . . . on the clout and flight ranges . . .

on the field archery course . . . on the hunting preserves . . . you couldn't find a single bow made of wood, other than my own. Metal bows were a brief rage at the start of this revolution but were speedily followed by glass bows (glass as in glass fishing rods), composite shooting tools made of laminated strips of aluminum and maple and plastic, and finally that cantilevered product, now omnipresent, which to me looks as if it was contrived by an orthodontist in traction, after consultation with the Roeblings and a suggestion from Rube Goldberg.

The same thing happened to arrows. The only arrows in existence in the 1920s were wooden ones, ranging from the clumsy birch dowel to the finest matched set of Port Orford cedar. The best set of wooden arrows I ever owned was guaranteed to group in the bull's-eye at sixty yards, and of course it did. But the twelve individual members of the set wouldn't group in the same *part* of the gold, which is the nine-inch bull's-eye. I took my new set to my own range and shot them throughout one afternoon, setting down on paper the pattern of each group shot. It soon began to emerge that arrow # 1 flew high and left to eleven o'clock in the gold; arrow # 2 had an attraction for three o'clock, and so on. Why, the dozen had a pattern five or six inches wide at sixty yards, and that would never do. So I memorized my numbered arrows, and made the necessary tiny allowances when shooting. So did everybody else, with his set. Even when dealing with the finest material and the finest craftsmanship, identity was impossible with wood.

Wooden arrows shortly became almost curiosities—as extinct on the tournament field as wooden-shafted golf clubs on the links. Aluminum alloy, tubular steel, and glass became the thing. My metals—yes, I succumbed to them in self-defense—still group, not merely in the gold, but in a half-dollar. They are not closely approximate but almost identical, in weight and spine. Each one does exactly what the other one does, provided only that the archer gives it a chance.

You will have gathered from my tone of voice that I do not like this evolution, that to my mind only the wooden longbow is a thing of beauty and joy forever. You are right. To me, no modern bow has a personality, much less a soul. I admit they will shoot. They will outshoot any wooden bow ever made. If you want to get out on the tournament line and shoot for keeps with the other boys and girls, you have to use these bows. They can be held steady with minimal strain at full draw; they are unaffected by heat and humidity; they won't let down or build up in power as the hours pass; they simply stay in there and shoot each arrow exactly as the one before it—or so I am told. Yew bows, on the contrary, are so sensitive to atmosphere and heat that if a heavy cloud passes across the sun the cast of the bow can be different from one end to the next. Yes, I do regret our ingenious propensity for taking the romance out of romance. If modern archery is seeking to recapture romance, even to protest against the mechanization of life, how strange that it does so with machine-made instruments.

Let's stop frothing at the mouth and get back to "early" archery, where I feel at home. What about the accuracy of the bow and arrow, in the hands of an expert, even back in those good old days? Put it this way: Years ago I gave up using my best arrows at distances less than forty yards because it was too destructive. You Robin-Hooded too many arrows—split one with the other. Lacking that, you smashed one against the other with the vibration as they fell into the target side by side.

Or put it this way: I've seen a former national champion shoot an arrow through a cardboard poker chip at twenty yards, then put a second arrow through the same hole. This fellow wasn't winning the big tournaments any more. He wasn't good enough.

Or again: For winter work, to keep muscles in trim and to maintain competition, the Olympic Round was devised—ninety arrows to a standard four-foot target at thirty yards, a distance readily available indoors. Since the gold counts nine points, a perfect score is 810. I once watched a friend, O. K. Smathers of Brevard, North Carolina, shoot an 808 in the basement of Asheville's city hall. That's 89 arrows in the gold, with one strayed off into the red. Smathers was then the best target shot in North

Carolina, and in fairly short order went on to become world champion. Presently much older and retired, with knees fractured as the result of an accident, he's still a formidable archer.

Thirty yards is mighty close work, of course. The sixty yards, fifty yards, and forty yards shot outdoors in the American Round—thirty arrows at each distance—provide a better test of skill than the indoor Olympic. Yet perfect ends—all six arrows in the gold—occurred in this event also. They were noteworthy, but they happened. If memory serves, Ree Dillinger once had to shoot a perfect end on the final target in order to win the national championship.

A double American Round used to be our standard tournament event; we'd shoot one in the morning and another in the afternoon. In local events that sufficed to let you know who was the best archer. However, the ancient York Round, devised in England centuries ago, provided a better test of skill. It was used at the larger and more important meetings to separate the men from the boys. In the York Round the first seventy-two arrows are shot from one hundred yards, the next forty-eight from eighty yards, and the last twenty-four from sixty yards. When you finished a double York Round you had excellent evidence as to who was the best shot. It is rather easy to miss the entire target from one hundred yards. Perfect ends aren't often shot at that distance. In fact, I've never seen one made, although I've seen the next thing to it.

Let me try to give you some idea of the precision required in tournament target archery, illustrated by a sorry spectacle I once made of myself at one hundred yards. I was using my beloved yew bow although it had no business performing at that distance, as it had been built for the American Round. But I liked it, so I shot it, underpowered as it was.

Shooting technique, when using point-of-aim on the ground rather than a sight on the bow, calls for placing your right hand—your string hand—firmly under your chin as a fixed base and sighting over the point of your arrow. I found, this warm day, that when my eye and the point of the arrow and the gold of the target were in direct line, the arrow fell short of its mark. That left me with a choice of evils. I could aim the point of the arrow higher, say at a leaf on a tree above the target; or I could drop my right hand below my chin, getting greater elevation either way. I didn't fancy aiming at a leaf shimmering in the breeze at that distance, so I put a small block of wood, about an eighth of an inch thick, between my back teeth, thus depressing my chin slightly, and found that when I then aimed at the gold I hit the gold—all other things being equal. And so the tournament started.

A few ends later my first arrow fell short, hitting the ground some yards in front of the distant target. A thing like that evokes furious thinking. Has the bow let down? No, the heat's about the same. Did you flinch or punch? Were you off your point of aim? No. It was probably your release. You dragged the string a bit instead of letting it get sharply away. Careful on the next one; you've just tossed away nine points. So I was careful with the next arrow, and again it fell short.

Now the inner struggle really begins. You examine your bow, your string, your arrows. You test the breeze. You estimate the heat and the humidity. You break down and ask your competitors how they're doing. Alas, they're doing very well indeed. You decide, therefore, to resist the impulse to aim higher.

Look, you counsel yourself, trust your form. Don't get panicky. Relax. Shoot as well as you can, and don't even look up to follow the flight of your arrow. That way lies madness.

So I shot the rest of the end with infinite care and without looking up, faithful to the advice of my inner coach. When I walked up to the target I found one of the finest groups I had ever shot, a lovely tight one clustered on the ground five yards short. And only then did I realize what you have probably long since figured out— that I had forgotten to put that little sliver of wood between my teeth that end. Thus it was I learned, the hard way, that with that particular bow and set of arrows on that particular day, an eighth of an inch difference in elevation became magnified, at one hundred yards, into a difference of five yards of distance and four feet in height—the center of a target is four feet off the ground.

In our context of accuracy the moral of this is: don't let anybody, no matter how good, shoot a cigarette from between your lips, no matter how short the distance is. It can indeed be done, and it has been done. But the world's best isn't going to do it to me. I know too much about the big differences that little differences make.

From another angle, the episode illustrates the intense concentration required on the tournament field, which ultimately led me to abandon that aspect of the sport. As I grew older, as my life became more complex and demanding, I began to think about a less taxing hobby. My very tackle-box began to accuse me. Like all archers I carried to the tournaments a tackle-box as big as a foot locker, full of range finders and foot markers and sights and prisms and shooting-gloves and beeswax and extra strings (much of the time) and what-not. One day I took a good sober look at that box and was reminded of the preface to the first English Prayer Book, which stated, in reference to the inordinately complicated orders of service existing before its composition, that "many times there was more business to find out what should be read, than to read it when it was found out." Whereupon I gave up target archery. From that day forward I have simply thrown my quiver on my back, picked up my bow, and stepped out into the woods.

TEN

The Deerslayer

I must have resembled a pretzel . . .

The first time I went deer hunting with bow and arrow I couldn't find the forest; five o'clock in the morning is always a confusing time to me. I chased that elusive patch of woods for a fruitless hour. When it was light enough to see, I was driving aimlessly down a forgotten road, and there I came upon my first human being—a local character, I thought, presumably out to milk his cows or make corn liquor, or whatever those hillbillies do.

It happens, though, that I had stumbled on Bill Casselberry, and he soon set me straight in my directions. Bill knew every foot of the Bent Creek watershed that I was trying to locate. It was his business to, for he owned a guest ranch in the neighborhood, and his riding trails wandered through the whole game preserve. I was happy to see him.

He joyfully abandoned the trail-grading that he had possibly been thinking about doing and crawled into my car to act as pilot. As we clattered along, he indicated my archery tackle and asked, "You going hunting with those things?"

"Yes," I said, with considerable dignity.

Bill, I learned subsequently in one of life's fine friendships, often has nothing to do except needle inoffensive people. Right then, in any case, he grated out what might have been a laugh and said, "Well, aren't you the damn fool."

I was hurt, but I swallowed my pride and proceeded to lecture Bill. I reminded him of Crécy and Agincourt, when the English clothyard shaft penetrated armor front to back, including the unfortunate Frenchman inside. I told him that the American Indians used to kill buffalo, and not with their fists. I recounted the exploits of Art Young and Saxton Pope, who had successfully investigated the possibility of killing lions and suchlike with the bow. I stopped the car to shave my arm for him with the edge of a broadhead—and was rather pleased when the razor-sharp thing cut me. Warming to my work, I assured him truthfully that killing bear, moose, elk, panther, boar, and deer with arrows was a commonplace; that the hobby was respectable because Erle Stanley Gardner was an archer; and that Howard Hill had slain a fifty-foot whale with one shot. I threw the whole book at him, but when I ran out of breath he was still unconverted.

"Deer move faster than whales," he said. "Besides, they're smaller. You're still a damn fool."

"I'll come back to your place and prove it to you," I told him as I put the car into gear.

"Don't need proof," he said meanly. "Believe it already." Then—perhaps it was the hurt look on my face—he relented. "Tell you what," he stated. "I'll show you a couple of places to hunt. And you stay at my ranch until you get your deer."

I wish I had that offer in writing, the cost of living being what it is.

At the ranger station I handed over my hunting license. That license, incidentally, was North Carolina Permit Number One. And

96

nobody had applied for Number Two—this was the state's first bow hunt. For three days I was to have the 100,000-odd acres of Pisgah National Forest all to myself, with lots of deer for company.

I pondered that fact after Bill had put me on a stand in an open meadow and left me to my meditations. "There'll be a deer by here this morning, like as not," he had said, so I began to imagine the headlines that would appear under my picture in the paper: "Local man is first to kill deer with bow and arrow in Pisgah Forest since the day of the Cherokee Indians." That seemed somewhat long for a headline, but I thought they might possibly run it. The editor of the paper and several of its reporters were parishioners of mine now that I was rector of an Asheville parish.

A couple of hours later it dawned on me that Bill undoubtedly loved a practical joke. A brief walk put me on another stand of my own choosing, and there Bill found me asleep shortly before noon.

"There's a deer grazing in the meadow where I had you," he told me.

"Oh," I said.

Bill took me to another stand, near a salt lick, and this time he stayed around to keep an eye on me. About two o'clock he stretched and broke the silence. "Deer aren't moving around much today," he said, sagely.

I agreed, in a tone that tried to put the blame where it belonged.

Bill blandly failed to get it. He sat up, scratched, looked my equipment over, and said "Let's see you shoot." He pointed out a sapling fifty yards away; a sprout nearly two inches thick. "See the patch of grey about two feet up that dogwood?"

I could just make out the starveling tree itself, let alone the alleged spot of lichen, but of course there was only one thing to do. With Bill breathing over my shoulder, I took aim and loosed. The arrow sped true and struck home, obviously in the center of the proper spot.

Bill pushed back his moth-eaten hat. Although he said nothing, he seemed impressed, not to say amazed. So was I.

97

Happily, the little feat seemed to galvanize Bill into activity, for he managed to get on his feet and lead me along a woods path in the hope of stirring up a deer. When we rounded the second bend in the path, he stopped short. "There's a deer in there," he said casually, over his shoulder.

I crowded close. "Where?"

"Under that sourwood tree. Not ten feet away. Standing there just looking at us."

For thirty seconds I craned and peered. "Where?" I asked again.

He pointed. "There. By the sourwood."

A sourwood meant nothing to me, so I looked along his outstretched arm. "I don't see it," I had to say after a while.

Bill hooked his thumbs through his belt loops. "Well, I doubt if he'll stand there all day," he said, as to a child.

It seemed a reasonable opinion, so, remembering the lichen on the dogwood tree, I resolved just to shoot in the general direction. As if the phantom animal had suddenly become visible, I quickly raised my bow. Perhaps that movement was what made the deer jump out and whisk around the corner. Oh, yes, there was a deer there, right by the sourwood tree. It was a nice-looking deer, so I ran after it. But my heavy hunting boots probably slowed me down; besides, the deer had a head start.

When I came back to the path, Bill asked, "Catch him?" At my shake of the head he laughed, not in a pleasant manner, and ambled away. I followed, without further conversation, for perhaps a quarter of a mile. And then I saw a deer. I saw it first. It was about thirty yards away, broadside to us, and apparently not aware of our presence. I took careful aim and shot.

We found the arrow forty feet up in a pine tree, stuck solidly in a thick branch. I unlimbered my quiver and Bill boosted me to a lower limb so that I could climb up and retrieve it.

"One trouble with bow hunting in these thick woods is that your arrow can ricochet off branches," I explained.

"That's one trouble," Bill agreed, accenting the second word.

Within a mile, we turned a corner and came upon a herd of half a dozen deer, grazing in an old quarry. They immediately bounded off in all directions, with the exception of one that elected to stand there and watch us.

The deer was a long eighty yards away, so I stalked it for five minutes with the greatest care. I bent over into a half crouch, held my breath, and moved my feet so carefully that not a leaf stirred. It must have been quite an impressive performance, for the deer, which was watching me all the time, never budged.

I had closed the gap to about forty yards when Bill, behind me, bawled out, "That one isn't gonna stand there all day either."

I straightened up quickly, turned around, and waved violently at him. "Quiet, will you!" I bellowed. "You'll scare him!"

Chastened, Bill subsided, and I resumed my stealthy approach until I had achieved a clear shot from thirty yards' distance. Then I stood erect, measured off the distance with my trained eye, raised my bow, took long steady aim, and loosed carefully.

It was a beautiful shot, like the one that had hit the dogwood. Any experienced archer will assure you truthfully that he can tell the final destination of an arrow the moment it leaves his bow, and this particular arrow was on the deer's heart all the way. It is unfortunate, therefore, that at the last moment a twig reached down and deflected the speeding shaft. I think that the arrow was no more than ten feet from the deer when it glanced aside and thundered into an oak tree that stood just in front of the deer's nose.

Stimulated, the animal drifted up the hillside for twenty yards and skylined himself, presenting a huge expanse of broadside as he stopped to look back. I reached around for my quiver, but unfortunately it wasn't there. I had left it under that pine tree.

While I was occupied in digging my broadhead out of the tree, Bill, who was occupied in digging his toe into the ground, told me that he had just remembered some important business back at his ranch. Before leaving, however, he did speak about an old orchard that was a bit farther along the road, so after retrieving my quiver I established myself there in the lower branches of a gnarled apple tree. Surely, I thought, the deer couldn't see or scent me ten feet off the ground.

Less than half an hour later, a pair of does sauntered into the orchard and grazed to my tree. I was right, for without any doubt they didn't know that I was within miles. When they finally departed, twenty minutes or so later, I was so pleased with my hunting instincts I decided to toast myself from my thermos bottle.

The coffee was still hot. In fact, it was so hot that I had to slurp it noisily in order to get it past my lips. The thunder of hoofs at the noise of my drinking made me spin around fast enough to see two bucks, which had been browsing unnoticed behind me, bound off and disappear into the forest. Also I fell out of the tree.

It was getting late anyway, so I went back to Bill's ranch. "Didn't get another shot," I said before Bill could open his mouth—and that is no mean feat. "Tomorrow, how about showing me a decent place to hunt?" I added.

Our further conversation that night is not worth reporting.

The next day it turned bitterly cold, and the account of my hunting is short. I didn't see a deer all day. This I can say, however—twelve hours is a long, cold time to be sitting on a stump.

On the third and last morning it was raining a steady and particularly damp drizzle. For about an hour I stood high on a ridge overlooking acres of thin woods, wondering why one's manhood has to be proved out in the open in dreary November. I wondered what remarks Bill would make this time. I wondered how long it took pneumonia to develop and how a nice case felt. Every thirty seconds I blew a drop of water off the end of my nose.

Then I heard my subconscious say, "Look, God. The way I heard it You're supposed to bring the more abundant life. Yet here I've frozen for one day, and now I'm drowning, which is surely not the life abundant. And Bill is waiting back at the ranch. I'd like You to send me a deer. Not a little old doe, either. A great big buck with a rack of horns. Or at least one visible spike."

For five minutes I stood there, staring down the still empty ridge, or watching the rawhide slowly give way to the rain and peel off the back of my bow, or wondering how often my plaintive hunter's prayer had crept whining into Heaven under similar circumstances.

I had just blown away another drop of water when the hunch came—the ghostly intrusion that we all get from time to time. "Better look over your shoulder," it said. "But look around slow."

Obediently, I turned my head slowly, and there stood my buck. Broadside to me, not twenty feet away, quietly looking me over without much observable interest.

I must tell you about that buck—I talked him over with Bill afterwards. It was the legendary buck of Pisgah Forest, a huge grey-blue beast with a rack of horns like Santa Claus's reindeer, and quite the biggest deer that anybody has ever seen. Bill told me of the time, three years before, when he had found one of the animal's horns, which at that time carried six points. I myself counted eighteen points that morning, nine on a side. There was plenty of time to count.

Bill also told me that particular buck lived up and down the ridge that I happened to be on and could be found there at any time of the year except during the hunting season. Time and again he had seen the deer on the day before the guns went off and on the day after the cease-fire order, but never in the interval between. Once, on a bet, he had actually taken a party of disgruntled and disbelieving hunters to that empty ridge two days after the season closed, and there lay the buck, massive and placid as a cow, watching from the side of the road.

So there we were, the legendary buck and I, staring into each other's eyes. As the drop of water formed again on my nose, I wondered what to do. To jump around quickly—of course I was facing in the wrong direction—drawing as I jumped and letting the arrow fly before I hit the ground? No. The buck was younger and spryer than I by some thirty years and undoubtedly could jump much faster. I even had the feeling that he would know the very moment when my muscles tensed for the leap, so I dismissed the idea.

To turn around slowly, imperceptibly? Yes. That was what they told you to do in the books I had read.

So I started to turn. My upper body had pivoted about a quarter of the way when the buck solved my dilemma for me. With disdainful indifference he averted his head and looked up the ridge. I couldn't see his eyes any longer, and therefore he couldn't see me. All I could see was the inverted rocking chair that he carried on his head.

Don't tell me what I should have done. I know now, better than you do. I have done the stunt nightly for months in my disturbed sleep, and in each dream my arrow has cut him down. I should have jumped around on those silent leaves and let him have it. He wouldn't have known what hit him.

What I actually did, however, was accelerate my rate of slow turning. When I finally got into such a position that I must have resembled a pretzel, the deer turned back on cue, laughed out loud at my contortions, flicked his tail once, and rollicked off down the hill into a laurel thicket.

I never got the arrow off. But I did send something after him. And if you will forgive me for being the one who says it, the epithets were extremely well chosen.

A couple of hours later, in another part of the forest, I found a splendid game trail commanded at one point by a tall evergreen tree. I crawled into the tentlike haven provided by the drooping lower branches and proceeded to construct the best blind that has ever been known to man. When I was through, I could turn noiselessly and invisibly in every direction and shoot readily through half a dozen gaping loopholes I had made.

"Now let 'em come," I said aloud through teeth that chattered. "And God help 'em when they do!"

Perhaps thirty minutes later, they came. Not one buck but two came mincing down the trail. I readied myself and let them come. It seemed to take two hours, but perhaps it was closer to two minutes that I endured their leisurely approach. Now they were twenty yards away, now ten yards, and finally the first buck was a mere ten feet distant. With another step he would be opposite my best loophole and not eight feet from me. Swiftly I raised my bow.

This seems the best place to say a few words about building a blind when hunting deer with bow and arrow. In addition to all that I had done, it is also important to clear the branches to a distance of three feet above your head. This is essential—I am entirely dogmatic on the point. If you fail to do so, the top of your upflung bow knocks against an overhead branch, the slight shock bumps your arrow off the string, and the ensuing unearthly disturbance sends the deer hurtling down the hillside like a locomotive. The chances are extremely good that you will not even note the direction in which escape is made. The deer will simply disappear.

But to get back to our hunting. As the dreary day slogged toward its end, I found a fallen log astride a well-marked trail, and there I sat down wearily. I set my bow beside me on the log, smoked a limp and dispirited cigarette, and then took out my handkerchief to wipe my glasses. I had started on the second lens when a spike buck broke out of the rhododendron about forty yards away and began trotting down the trail toward me. His head was down. He did not see me sitting there across his path.

Yes, I know what I should have done. I should have sat there immovably until he hopped the log, six feet to my left. Then I could have dropped my handkerchief and glasses, swooped up my fallen bow, and probably got in a shot from my sitting position. All that I know, now.

When I let fall my handkerchief while the deer was still thirty yards away, thus waving a large white flag before his eyes, his head come snorting up, his legs exploded him into the woods at my right, and my pursuing arrow shattered on a branch.

There are lessons to be derived from my experiences in the role of deerslayer. Things like these: jump around quickly; don't move a muscle; never wipe your glasses; don't wear glasses; clear out the brush; stay well hidden; never sit down; and many others. The major part of this winter I shall devote to sorting out all these items and arranging them in alphabetical order.

For of course I am going hunting again. I am going forty-nine more times. The statistics say that one archer in fifty gets his buck. So that wizened oldster you will find at the end of the century, sitting in his camouflaged wheelchair high on a ridge in the lengthening shadows, will be me.

Bill Casselberry will not be sitting there (in the flesh) by my side. He died, of leukemia, a quarter-century ago and less than a decade after I had first met him roaming the depths of Pisgah Forest. He will reappear now and again in these pages, however, because all unknowingly he helped orient me in the midst of several other woods and remains forever in my thoughts. In fact I am writing these words at his lovely, vast, antique desk which the lady who had been his wife gave me when, a few years after Bill's death, she became a nun.

Sometimes I think that a Requiem Eucharist exerts the Church's second most powerful missionary force. Certainly Bill's funeral had that effect upon those merry men and women, the Asheville Archers, who attended it in a body. Subsequently "my" parish—more truly Bill's parish, for he and his family had affiliated there—spontaneously became their unofficial spiritual home, just as his ranch had long been the center of gravity, and of levity, for their—for our—spirited hobby. Many of us had been his guests there during the hunting seasons and at other times. He had encouraged us to build our roving range throughout his woodlands. He had bulldozed a meadow into a vast target range to be headquarters for our weekly tournaments, for our annual set-to with the Cherokee Indians, and for the Southeastern Championships, all of which he entertained lavishly. In brief, he had turned us loose on his domain, with admonitions against mistaking one of his horses for deer. Bill did not live to know the fact, but he had thus attracted not a few souls toward the Kingdom of Heaven.

Incidentally, in my prejudiced view the Church's third most powerful missionary force is a good boarding school, whether that school be one for boys or for girls or for both. I could easily document the contention statistically, but we'll let it pass in order to hurry on and single out the Church's primary and supreme missionary power—the laity; Bill and others like, but of course each one totally unlike, him. In fact, the laity *is* the Church, and the Church is God's mission.

I suspect that individual laypeople (like Bill) do not realize their missionary power and indeed "do not believe in missions." With their own identities achieved, or at least rooted and grounded sufficiently securely, they so respect individuality that they feel no compulsion to convert others to their own persuasion; no itch to direct the lives of others. They simply radiate around themselves the compelling aura of mature stability. The result is a powerful attraction to the source of that strength. So it was not really Bill's untimely death and funeral that had missionary effect. It was Bill's vibrant life. His hearty, outgoing, self-forgetful, thoughtful, generous, and, above all, loving life had continually burst its own confines and overflowed into the others around him. His Requiem focused that fact, so those others stood in awe, each realizing how truly this man was a son of God.

ELEVEN

Horse Sense

. . . you don't sit a horse as you do a chair.

Equitation is an ancient and storied art, a demanding and intricate science, a complex and beautiful skill, about which I know absolutely nothing. It is practiced by equestrians in queer clothes— gentry with the leisure and lucre to pursue horsemanship as almost a career in itself. They're all lovely folk, as everyone knows, but their photographs in the slick magazines at your dentist's office can portray them (and their horses) with patrician noses acquired in looking down at us peasants. You yourself have considered riding, but their jodhpurs and mystique have scared you away.

Fortunately there really is such a thing as plain old horseback riding, enjoyed by us folk who were raised when a horse was primarily a means of conveyance. Riding a nice tame one has since become good fun and exercise for both man and beast. As it happens I'm going over to Bill's ranch for an hour's ride as soon as I finish hoeing this row of beans. You come along and try it, my way. I think I can teach you the essentials, if the equestrians will stay outta here.

Clothes? I'm going to wear what I've got on. Your blue jeans, sneakers, and old flannel shirt will be just fine.

Here at the stable, personally confronted by a horse, you face a moment of truth. A horse is big and formidable enough at a distance; up close he is huge and menacing. An alarming amount of white gives a wicked gleam to his eye as he looks ponderously around to inspect you while you gaze soberly back, moodily surveying the horse's aspect. The leer on his face is clearly sardonic, with overtones of ominous patience. You see in one glance that this horse does not like you. You are certain that if he permits you to get up onto him it will only be so that he can then dissect you at leisure.

Don't go back home. Trust me when I say that in reading a horse's character from his external appearance you are involved in the pathetic fallacy. Every horse has a lot of white in his eye simply as a gift of nature. Nature gave him that sardonic look and those wicked yellow teeth. All this may not mean a thing. You can never be entirely certain until it is too late, of course, but the odds are a hundred to one that he is thoroughly broken in, non-neurotic, philosophical, and quite tired. If it were otherwise, Bill would sell him for glue. He really would. Repeat business is what brings in the hay, oats, and gravy, and hospitalized customers make for poor repeat business.

To clinch my case I offer this practical example. The first time I approached a horse at public hire the animal promptly lowered its head, opened its mouth a foot, bared dreadful fangs, and snarled. Naturally I quailed, for unless the unfortunate beast had swallowed a grapefruit which it was trying to dislodge by inverse suction, it was obviously measuring the calf of my leg for size. The fit was evident.

From behind a handy tractor I inquired of the animal's master, "What's he doing that for?"

"He's just yawnin'," the fellow said, and spat. "Hoss is plumb sleepy. Mebbe you kin stir 'im up a bit."

He didn't seem very hopeful about this possibility, so I went ahead with my plans. Events proved he was right. I couldn't stir the hoss up at all, which was just fine with me.

If I have persuaded you to mount your animal, walk to the creature's left side. (There's a longstanding convention about this. I'll bet we can get on from the other side if we want to, but it appears to be better not to want to. The cowboys, along with the horsey set, say the left-hand side, so let's do it their way.) Put your left foot into the stirrup you will find hanging there, grab the seat of the saddle with both hands, and prepare to heave skyward.

The horse will now immediately start walking away, leaving you in a sad predicament. Your left foot is three feet off the ground, firmly clutched in that unyielding stirrup, yet you are in implacable sidewise motion. Some cynics will have it that the horse employs this gambit on purpose, and it may be so. You are indeed a piteous sight as you hop along on your right foot, obviously terrified lest the horse pin it firmly to the ground and then split your personality. However, there is little evidence that horses have a sense of humor—or much sense of any kind, for that matter—and, in fact, your situation is more embarrassing than dangerous. Sooner or later you should simply fall down, pick yourself up, get the attendant to hold the horse fixedly in one spot, and try again.

This time, if you are able-bodied at all, you will find yourself up there, facing across the horse's back. You will then be able to get your other leg over the saddle and your right foot down into its stirrup.

What if you can't? Have the attendant hoist you. He's done it for others before you, and he'll do it for those who come after. You don't have to ask him what his thoughts are. Since he is in business and wisely laconic, he will not tell you unasked.

I have a glorious vision of you up there in the saddle, a long way off the ground. You are finding that this unimagined eminence produces a curiously mingled sensation of insecurity and power. You yearn to cringe down toward Mother Earth, but at the same time you know you'll take a good picture if you sit up even higher.

Concentrate on that last half of the feeling; the swagger is part of what you're paying for. While you're getting used to the altitude, you can stall for time by having your lackey adjust the stirrups. Notice how he locates the rusted buckle that permits this adjustment and the length of stirrup he leaves. If he does it correctly, as many of them do, the stirrup will bump against your ankle bones when your feet are hanging free from them. This amount of stirrup elevation makes you feel somewhat secure when your feet are actually in the stirrups, and these intervals do increase with practice.

Of course you will want to embrace the stirrups lovingly with your insteps, but a moment's reflection on your predicament if you fell off while thus in irons will change your mind in a hurry. Hold the bottom of the stirrup across the ball of your foot, about where your big toe begins. Keep your toes up and out and your heels down and in, say at a comfortable (?) thirty-degree angle.

The amount of pressure you put into the stirrups is different at different times, so don't bother me with foolish questions about that. Let's move our attention up higher. Keep your knees pressed against the nether parts of the saddle, but don't hope for a scissor-grip around the horse. I realize that such a grip sounds like a swell idea, but it is physically impossible. I've tried.

Coming up still higher, we arrive at the most ludicrous part of the human anatomy. It isn't too useful in riding because you don't sit a horse as you do a chair; you sit on your unborn generations. Roll yourself into that position. Some of you, all too obviously, will now be sticking out behind. It will simply have to. Riding a horse hadn't been thought of when the human fanny was evolved. Just hollow your back, relax the rest of you, and there you are.

Assuming that you have actually achieved all this, look down now. An imaginary plumb line dropped from your eyes ought to skim your knees and your toes. Beyond question your feet are sticking out in front of that line, groping for the brakes, so get them back. You really can do better in this more rearward position, although I didn't believe it at first, either.

Those worn leather thongs you have been clutching are the reins, of course. Keep them firmly in both hands.

I grant you it's a many-splendored thing to sit a horse, or even to ride one, holding the reins with one hand while the other swings carelessly free or rests rakishly akimbo. Either attitude makes you feel singularly devil-may-care, so by all means pose in this manner before motion is achieved, if you want to. However, when actually riding, you'll be more in control and steer better with the reins held securely in both hands. Just ball them into loose fists with their backs up in the nearly natural position and the reins emerging between forefinger and thumb. You then steer in the obvious manner. Perhaps I had better remind you to let up with one hand when you pull with the other, lest your horse become so confused and frustrated that he sits down to have a good cry.

Unfortunately, that isn't quite all there is to steering, partly because even the most imbecilic horse has an inner life of his own. Strange things go on under the hood. For example, sometimes a horse entertains personal opinions about the destination in view. You, in hot pursuit of a chosen objective, are diligently pulling toward the right. The horse's head indeed comes around in that direction, to the extent that you hastily withdraw your foot lest it be gnawed on, but the rest of the animal keeps going crabwise down the road. This is embarrassing, frustrating, and even alarming if a truck is bearing down on you.

"Don't let the horse get away with that!" they always screamed at me when I was in this fix. "Teach him who's boss! You're on top, aren't you?"

I refer the advice to you, emphatically but in a low tone of voice; experience has proved that shouting serves only to compound a bad situation. The horse is indeed the lower animal, in both senses, and it is wise to keep things that way. Human dignity is at stake. Do try to make him go in the direction you have chosen, even if it was a bum decision in the first place. Keep the reins pulled back hard— not out wide the way you're doing it but toward you and upward, and with as short a hold as you can manage. Boot the beast in the ribs, again and again. Eventually he'll come around or, alas, you will.

Now that we stand on the dread threshold of locomotion, let's decide right away to walk the horse for a while. There are various good reasons for this. A horse is a thing of flesh and blood, like a baseball pitcher, so it's easier on him to loosen up slowly and gradually. In addition, a sedate beginning gives him time to take you philosophically. You yourself will be a more balanced personality at a walk—but what am I going on like this for? Your passion to walk your horse is far fiercer than my desire that you should.

To set things in motion, loosen and jiggle your reins (you've been holding them grimly tight), lightly kick your heels against the horse's ribs (there goes a stirrup), murmur something hopeful, and your horse should start.

If he merely readjusts his ears, ask the attendant for a little switch. Better still, pull one off a tree yourself with all nonchalance, as if you knew from long experience how to take care of the situation. The mere crackle of a breaking twig will usually do the trick because a seasoned horse is a realist who knows all about switches. However, if he doesn't start shambling at this warning, apply your switch *lightly* to the part of the horse behind the saddle. Now you're off. I mean, you're away, walking down the road.

If you can still cerebrate at this point, pay a thought to your hands. Stop holding those reins tightly back or you'll numb the horse's mouth, making him uncomfortable now and unresponsive later—an undesirable situation, and I don't mean merely for the horse. Keep them loose but without much slack, holding your hands low and in front of the saddle, not up and back around your belt line. In this forward position you're holding with that short rein you hear about. It gives plenty of open space to pull back into, which is an extremely useful option for you to keep open.

Now let your hands move loosely back and forth with the natural nodding motion of the horse's head—keeping your hands on the horse's neck for a while will give you the rhythm. This motion is as professional as can be, and therefore will be satisfying to your ego. Some claim that, being professional, it also serves to give a horse the illusion that you're an old hand at the game, thus creating in him a misplaced confidence in you. I doubt it. In my opinion the horse is happy that his mouth isn't being pulled to pieces at every step and responds with gratitude. He sized you up correctly the moment he first saw you.

Before we go any further, it will be an excellent idea to reveal how to stop this juggernaut you have set in motion. You merely pull back firmly and evenly on the reins with both hands, bracing your feet into the stirrups so that you don't wind up on the horse's neck or even in the road. It's as simple as that. About the only mistake you can make is to haul back too hard and too far. A light pressure will do the trick, whereas pulling too hard can lead to a truly astonishing result—a frenzy of rearing, snorting, and sidestepping on the horse's part as the bit cuts into his mouth.

You can, of course, audibly mention something about stopping if that makes you feel any better. The horse will come to a dead halt without any smooth talk, however. He's delighted with every chance to stand still and switch flies off himself.

When you have mastered the start, the walk, and the stop, we'll fire the booster rocket which moves the horse into a trot. It is only fair to warn you in advance that no beginner is ever prepared for the trot. It's the most incredible, and harrowing, gait a horse has. Just the same, when you think you're ready, loosen and jiggle the reins while the horse is walking. Shift your weight somewhat forward. Kick lightly with your heels. Maybe cluck or in some other audible manner plead with your steed to move on.

Assuming that he does, you are immediately stupefied and gasping, lost in the Dark Night of the Soul. You have hit the sound barrier and are caught in a shock wave, with horrible results. Your neck is snapping, your teeth are clicking, your elbows start flapping in the breeze, the reins fall out of your hands, and your left foot loses contact with its stirrup. You grab blindly for the front of the saddle, which is "pulling leather" and isn't cricket, but I certainly hope you succeed.

This whole nightmare has a simple anatomical cause. A horse has four legs, of course. When he trots he operates on a pair of them at a time; perhaps it is perversity which makes him select a front one and the opposite hind one. In any case, he pounds along in a see-saw manner, and you pound with him. It is more truthful to say you pound *against* him, as you have discovered.

The approved way out of this dilemma is to "post" while the horse trots. No horse has yet thought up a counterattack, so at this writing "posting" takes half the misery out of the fun you are having.

Grit your teeth and go into another trot, this time listening to the sound of the horse's hoofbeats. Say to yourself, "Up, Down, Up, Down, Up, Down" in rhythm to this sound, the while trying to reconcile the action of your fanny to this rhythm. (That other noise you hear is colonic and part of the Purgative Way. Disregard it.) Reconciliation is aided by leaning your weight forward, pushing heavily into the stirrups with your feet, gripping the horse a bit with your knees, and using your thigh muscles to lift yourself up and down with your knees as a pivot. All of this to the previously mentioned rhythm or a reasonable facsimile, which is the best that a neophyte can manage.

If you succeed, when you succeed, and to the degree that you succeed, you're posting. You will taste your success when your bottom begins to be beaten only half as often as before. You will savor it when you actually rise and descend with the horse in an amazingly fluid style, known theologically as the Illuminative Way. Even in moments of success, for a while you'll be flying high into the

114

air at every post. There'll be broad daylight between you and the saddle, with plenty of room for birds to fly around under there. But you'll come down again—although I hardly need to add that, for you are feeling at one with the startled lady who said, "You go up so *easy*, but you come down so *hard!*"

Because you can post a little now and then, let's fire the third stage and achieve orbital flight in the Unitive Way. It's called "cantering" in its beginning, relatively slow stage and "galloping" when the horse lays back its ears and really lets things rip, but you had better deny yourself that final privilege the first time out. It's more of a given thing than an achievement, anyway. Without meaning offense I'd say you had better wait until you and the horse are more at one than you presently appear to be; then the joy of ultimate union will be granted almost without your knowing it. For the nonce, then, while you are in a trot, shift your weight forward, kicking the horse in the ribs again—how this is done while posting, when your feet are otherwise occupied, is an excellent question—and an old rocking chair's got you. That nice, easy liquid motion is a canter. The torture of the trot is over, for man and beast. You are flowing easily up and down in slow motion while your horse covers ground. This is it; this is what you came out for. All you have to do now it keep your feet in the stirrups and relax—which is always more easily accomplished by thinking, "My, how nice it is to be relaxed!" than by ordering your nerves, your muscles, and your very soul to "Relax, damn you. Relax, I say!"

We can begin to gather up the fragments that remain by discussing, briefly, the Art of Jumping. My theory on jumping comes from an especially sound source—it was originated by a lady during her convalescence after making her horse jump a fence. To be more precise, the horse did not jump, but she did.

In a word the theory is "Don't."

Do have me notified should you decide to test it. Your stay in the hospital would give us opportunity to probe thoroughly into spiritual matters only hinted at here.

The more normal technique in dismounting is quite easy. Having found your way back to the stable whence you started—horses can do this unassisted—you come to your final stop and toss the reins to the attendant. While holding on with both hands to the front of the saddle, swing your right foot (minus its stirrup, for goodness' sake) over the horse's back to where your left foot is sustaining all your weight. Then lean forward so that your stomach supports you, and remove your left foot from its stirrup. From here you slip nicely to the ground.

Now try walking. Interesting, isn't it?

Nevertheless, walk to your car as steadily as you can. Drive home at the maximum legal speed, run a hot salt bath immediately, and lower yourself gratefully into it. This aftercare will make a world of difference, but even with the hot bath I'm afraid I know exactly how you will feel for a day or so, and where. You see, during the past hour you have rudely awakened certain muscles that have been slumbering for years. Tomorrow, and tomorrow, and tomorrow, they will exact their revenge.

TWELVE

Delightfully Unorthodox

Serge's eyes were out on stems.

What with Freud and his cohorts, not to mention the sequence of cause and effect, it seems reasonable to suspect that Dasha's childhood made her the kind of person she is today. Dasha's Russian family had been caught in the 1917 suction over there and made it to this country one leap ahead of the Bolsheviks. Then there followed many ennobling years spent in a brownstone house in New York City.

I can give you at second hand a few snatches of the life there. It seems that Dasha's mother, a queenly figure and indeed a genuine Russian princess, ran the gigantic four-story house which soon became a kind of refuge for other dispossessed Russian nobility. The clan gravitated there by centripetal force until whole boatloads of Russians were camped all over the place. Some came to stay until they found a job, and others because it was an inexpensive place for them to live until the job they had already found put them on their independent feet. Too usually the first class of visitors never found suitable employment, and most of the second class speedily managed to lose it, so there they just stayed.

The arrangement went on for years, presumably with Dasha's mother periodically selling some more crown jewels in order to make ends meet, but nobody seemed to mind. The counts and dukes were unfailingly cooperative, to hear Dasha tell it. Only occasionally was any of the guests at all testy, and that in a mild way. Perhaps as the clan trooped in to dinner after a particularly trying day, one of them might glance at the groaning table and mutter, "How . . . no wodka tonight?" But for the most part they were pretty decent about the whole thing.

Dasha doesn't know to this day how many of the Russian court were entertained in the brownstone house. Nobody knows. At least once a totally unexpected and unidentified guest was found in an isolated room on the fourth floor with evidence that he had been staying there for weeks. Nobody seemed to know when or whence he came, but he spoke Russian, and that was the password. The atmosphere of the whole establishment was, I gather, happy-go-lucky.

And then there was the night when the drunk got in the cellar. Dasha and her father were playing backgammon in the living room when they heard a gigantic crash from the basement. Dasha, understandably, sprang to her feet.

"First, we finish the game, Dasha," the old gentleman stated reprovingly. He impaled a long brown cigarette on the end of his telescopic holder and carefully lighted it. "After that is plenty of time to see what is happening."

If this attitude can be attained by means of revolution, Bolsheviks, and teeming brownstone houses, then perhaps these things have their place in civilization.

The scheduled investigation was indeed made after the backgammon game, and it seems that there was a drunken Italian in the cellar. There is no clue at all as to how he got there; his presence simply seemed appropriate to Dasha and her father, and I confess that it does to me too. The Italian was trying to get a huge Russian bed—one of the kind that sleeps fourteen at a pinch—out of a narrow cellar window, without visible success. I have not the faintest idea what his particular obsession was.

The prince, Dasha's father, took in the whole situation at a glance and bade the intruder a courtly good evening. "You have trouble, my friend," he observed.

The Italian admitted that he did, indeed.

"If you will go outside," the prince suggested, "I could then perhaps push from in here, and you could pull from out there. In that way . . ."

Apparently the notion seemed good to the befuddled Italian, who went happily outside, to appear shortly at the narrow slit of a cellar window. The prince and Dasha solemnly waved him goodbye, and went upstairs to start another game of backgammon.

I repeat that such things, plus devout Orthodox Christianity, have doubtless made Dasha what she is—capable, poised, serene, resourceful, hard-working, and determined to have fun along the way. So when she asked to be driven home after a diocesan planning session one afternoon— her husband Doug was tied up in a lengthy meeting, so she had come in a taxi—my wife and I were more than pleased. Whatever happened, and anything might, this was not going to be just another run-of-the-mill evening.

Home, it turned out, was not her place but ours. Dasha wanted to discuss a responsibility given her at the diocesan meeting before braving her own husbandless home, where Serge and Ivan and Tania were waiting to pounce on her. "First we finish the game. After that is plenty of time to see what is happening."

What was happening is a tangled story: Ivan was about to be married, for the third time, and of course he was in a highly nervous state. "For the third time" means here that the wedding had been put off when originally scheduled because the bride developed appendicitis and for the second time because she contracted mumps. If you have any understanding of impressionable young Russians, you will now have a clue to Ivan's state of mind the night before the third scheduled matrimonial attempt. I gathered that he wanted Dasha's imperturbable presence around him, both as a security blanket and to ward off measles.

Serge, on the other hand, had been expecting some friends from New York. He had been expecting them for three days. Daily he had made reservations for them at the Hilton; daily they had called him up from obscure off-route places to say that they would not be able to make it that particular night. Cancel the hotel reservations, please. But tomorrow they would arrive for sure. Make firm reservations for tomorrow. Then tomorrow came, as tomorrows do, but not Serge's guests. They too were Russians.

A series of calamities of this kind is enough to unsettle Serge completely. There is something in his orderly character that cannot cope with Fate on a rampage in the harrowing way that I have described. So Serge, too, desperately needed Dasha's calming personality. He also needed food, and Dasha was naturally the only person in the world who could provide it. Serge had doubtless heard of restaurants but apparently was unaware of their purpose. For seven years he had lived in that brownstone house.

Tania, the third impalee on a dilemma, was Dasha's business partner and as Russian and excitable as her name. There was something of vast moment she needed to discuss with Dasha— something complicated about valence boards for the Bishop's house, or an impasse of similar nature. I never found out exactly what it was—I asked the Bishop about it when I next saw him, but he didn't know. In any case Dasha was not interested in the problem at the moment. She thought it would keep. Certainly, what with Ivan, Serge and Tania lurking, Dasha was not quite ready to go home. She would discuss the diocesan matter for a few peaceful moments before departing to unsnarl three despairing lives.

Our telephone rang after we had learned of these things. It was for Dasha, from Serge—he had tracked her to our place through subtle detective work starting at the diocesan office we all had recently left together.

"They are coming!" he cried. My wife and I could hear him clear across the living room. "At last they are coming! They have only now telephoned again. They are but forty miles away!"

"Good," said Dasha. "I am so relieved. Good-bye."

"No . . . no!" Serge screamed. "Wait. There is more. I have not eaten! And they are not forty miles distant!"

"Eat, then," said Dasha. "Eat, and afterwards go meet them."

Serge's next remark was an incomprehensible shriek.

"But of course you can," Dasha said soothingly. "There are things to eat, and there is a can opener, and there is Tania. Tania knows about those things. She will fix you."

"Even so, then I have no way to go to the hotel," Serge wailed. He does not know about taxis.

"Why go to the hotel at all?" Dasha asked. "Telephone. Telephone the hotel and make reservations."

"I have called the hotel every day for three days. Maybe four days? I make reservations, then I break them. They are sick of me. Doubtless they would not honor this call. However, if I go in person—"

"Call a different hotel," Dasha counseled.

"The Hilton is the best in town," Serge's hauteur came across distinctly. "Do you forget that these are my guests?"

At this point Dasha had had enough. "Take my Buick," she said to Serge. Dasha owns no Buick. "Drive rapidly to Easthope." There is no such town hereabouts. "In the second Russian restaurant on the left you will get a fine meal. Charge it to me." Surely you know how many Russian restaurants there are in Easthope. "Then you can go personally to the Hilton and await your guests." She broke the connection, then called the Hilton and made Serge's reservation.

We ignored the subsequent ringing of my telephone, but this was no way to deal with Serge. After five minutes there was a knock at the door. It was Ivan, out of breath. He had run all the way from Dasha's house, just around the corner. A little muscle was twitching in his cheek. His eyes were haunted.

121

"Come home, Dasha," he implored. "Serge is beside himself. He cannot find the keys to the Buick. He cannot find the Buick."

"Everything is already fixed," Dasha assured him. "Be calm, Ivan. You also are beside yourself."

Ivan ran his hands through his wild hair. "I am being married," he whispered. "I am being married tomorrow, I hope. Dasha, tell me it will really happen this time."

"It will happen," she said.

I gave Ivan a drink. He sipped it morosely, still standing in the middle of the room. "Then tomorrow night I will be away from madness," he said at last. "Tomorrow night I will be on Amtrak to New York with Daria. We will sit side by side quietly and peacefully. All night long I will hold Daria's hand."

Dasha's eyebrows went up. "How is that?"

Ivan explained his outlandish honeymoon plans again.

Dasha rose. "Ivan, you will not! Ivan, think what you are saying!"

"It will be peaceful," Ivan sighed. "Peace, not madness."

"Look, Ivan," Dasha said. She put her hands on his shoulders. "Let me give you another wedding present. Let me order you a hotel room for tomorrow night—your wedding night, Ivan. You and Daria can sleep soundly and awake rested" (she kept her face impassive), "and you can go to New York the next day."

Ivan took a long slow sip of his drink. "Maybe that is good," he said at last. "I will call Daria's mother and ask her if she like the plan. You will make all the reservations, Dasha, please?"

However, we did not then learn what Daria's mother thought, for as Ivan went to the telephone the thing rang in his face. This time it was Tania. Serge, it seems, was nearly in tears.

"We will go," Dasha said to my wife as she hung up the phone. "We will go in five minutes. Ivan, run back. Tell Serge we are coming and meanwhile to do nothing." So Ivan went.

Dasha outlined her scheme, the telling of which gave Ivan enough time so that we would not pass him in my car, whereupon we followed. I opened the door of Dasha's house and stood aside so that my wife could support Dasha across the threshold.

"I'm all-ri'," Dasha murmured thickly. She swayed heavily against my wife, and the two staggered up the stairs.

I watched them go, then turned to the little semicircle of Tania, Serge, and Ivan. Tania's face was dead white. Serge's eyes were out on stems. The muscle in Ivan's cheek was beating like a pulse. They stared at me.

I spread my hands, sorrowfully shaking my head.

The four of us watched Dasha's heavy progress up the long stairs until finally Tania darted after. That broke the spell. Ivan clapped his hands to his head and collapsed onto a divan. Serge's shaking fingers inserted a cigarette into his long holder. "I have guests arriving," he muttered. He did manage a fair job of self-control until the hysterical laughter started coming down from above and Pushkin, Dasha's wolfhound, responded by tearing into the living room, scattering throw rugs in all directions, and bounded up the stairs in two vast leaps, howling questions in Russian.

Doug, Dasha's husband, chose that moment to get home from his meeting. "Hi," he said as he came in. "Glad to see you, and happy to be home. There's no place like home. Outside it's a jungle."

Pushkin, baffled by Dasha's closed door but heartened by a familiar voice from below, hurled himself down the stairs, shattering a lamp en route. Doug's six-two and two-twenty fended off the slavering monster. "It's good to be home," he repeated, "but not that good. Down, Pushkin. Settle down. Blamed dog only understands Russian. I don't know a word of it. Something's going on around here, I suppose."

It took me a while to explain, then to inform Serge that he was to go in Dasha's Ford—I handed him its keys—to the Hilton, which was expecting him, eat dinner there at a table reserved in his name, and there await his guests. However, the counsel finally penetrated, and I supported him to the car. He leaped in, snapped on the lights, speedily flooded the engine beyond all hope, but kept on grinding the starter. The headlights began to dim.

"Good God," Serge whispered hoarsely. In such a despairing tone he will doubtless acknowledge the Second Coming. He quit grinding the starter and slumped in his seat.

I slid in beside him, turned off the headlights, waited a bit, started the engine, and managed to leap out just in time. A thousand miles of hot rubber rasped off the rear tires, and Serge was gone, running without lights. I must suppose that he turned them on later. I went back into the house to eat sandwiches with Dasha, Tania, Doug, Ivan, Pushkin, and my wife. Tania, it turned out, is the kind that catches on fairly fast, Ivan has youth's resiliency plus infinite trust in Dasha, and Doug is always ready for anything. He has been married to Dasha for years.

There is little to add. Dasha of course succeeded in getting Ivan married the next day, and the idea about the hotel room did turn out to be well received. However, the Hilton had only one available room—the one Dasha had reserved for Serge's guests. Ivan and Daria spent their wedding night there, after Serge's guests had agreed, under the circumstances, to move into Dasha's house.

They are still there, and so is Serge. It looks to me as if the business of the brownstone house has started all over again. For my own selfish sake I hope so. A whole new batch of Orthodox Russians would do a lot for the neighborhood, for my parish, and even for the entire diocese.

THIRTEEN

Juniper Creek

*People are fine, but some days and
some places are better without them.*

Juniper Creek is a small run of crystal water that flows through the
"Yearling" country—that part of north-central Florida made famous
and familiar by Marjorie Rawlings. It ambles some twenty miles
from its source in the blue "boils" of Juniper Springs to its mouth in
Big Lake George and is one of the few streams in the world that are
navigable from end to end.

Of course "navigable" is a strong word as applied to Juniper
Creek. It describes far better the situation at the nearby, and better
known, Silver Springs, where good-sized vessels can and do cruise
to the very source: Silver Springs, where the headwater seems to be
actually deeper and wider than the magnificent Silver River that
flows from its springs to the Oklawaha River, and thence to the St.
John's, and thence to the Atlantic Ocean near Jacksonville. But I
use the word "navigable" about Juniper because it does apply to a

canoe and because it brings up a descriptive comparison with the widely known Silver Springs and Silver River. Juniper Springs and Juniper Creek are miniature, personalized, off-trail (in my day) editions of Silver Springs and Silver River. I say "in my day" because for seven years we lived nearby, having left Asheville to seek in Florida a climate conducive to our son's better health. "Jacob served seven years for Rachel; and they seemed unto him but a few days, for the love he had to her"—only in our case "her" was "him." After that most fruitful sojourn we were called back to North Carolina, in the inscrutable providence of God.

But let's get back to local geography. Juniper Spring is in the middle of the Ocala National Forest, about twenty-five miles south-east of the city of Ocala. Or, to look at it from our point of view when we lived there, fifty-five miles northwest of Daytona Beach. Or again, if one happened to be cruising Florida Highway 17, one turned west at Barberville and north at Astor Park.

We haven't lived in Florida for twenty-five years now, nor have we visited Juniper Creek during all that time, but I promise myself that we're going to someday soon, trusting that its unique charm has held up despite the population explosion. I expect that it has and that on a revisit we will once again step into serenity and beauty simply by wandering around the spring and the nature trail and the aquarium. Or picnicking in the lovely parks, amply provided by Uncle Sam with tables, shelters, and fireplaces. Or swimming, at any time of the year, in the incredible water of the spring—which was and surely is clearer than the air in the room where you are now sitting. We made sure to have swimming goggles, for the full effect.

During the years when we lived nearby we did all those things, when the spirit moved and our schedule permitted. But when we had a little more time, we took the canoe trip. How much time did one need for that? I imagine that a person could make the trip in about three hours if he wanted to set some kind of foolish record. The voyage covers the top fourteen miles of Juniper Creek, down-stream all the way, and given the compulsive neurosis that drives us Americans to cover the greatest distance in the shortest time, I am sure that some sweaty citizens have run the river in as brief a time as *two* hours. Some folk like to get there first if it kills them.

We liked to take all day. We'd roll into the park about eight o'clock in the morning, load our fishing gear, camera, lunch, cooler, and binoculars into the canoe, and shove off. We'd be back at the car by five or six o'clock in the evening.

By the way, where did the canoe come from? You could use your own, if you just happened to have an aluminum one with you—the occasional snags would probably tear a wood-and-fabric canoe to pieces in short order, although Juniper is the very opposite of a whitewater stream. However, Uncle Sam had two canoes available at the park, at three dollars per, and doubtless has many more available today, also doubtless at an inflated rental. We could have reserved one or both of those erstwhile canoes for a given date, and it might have been best to do so, in order to be sure. But we never bothered about that, and we were never disappointed. I will admit that we didn't go over there on weekends, and I suspect that things are different now.

The ranger helped us put the canoe into the water at a tiny rustic bridge below an old mill wheel where the creek was a mere trickle, perhaps five feet wide and six inches deep. He handed our impedimenta down to us. We'd forgotten to bring pillows, and we remembered that aluminum seats get awfully hard after a few hours, but the ranger had a couple of ancient cushions lying in the back of his pickup truck, so that was all right. He also provided the wooden frame, equipped with rubber suction-cups and ropes, that we'd use to bring the canoe back on the top of our car. He assured us that he'd have our car waiting for us, in plenty of time, at the bridge fourteen miles below.

"Keep your eyes open," he said as we drifted off. "Fellow and his wife went down yesterday and saw a couple of alligators and some deer."

At the first bend, ten yards downstream, we looked back to wave good-bye. The ranger was leaning on the railing of the bridge. "Good trip!" he called, lifting his hand. We looked forward again to steer around the bend, and from that time on we had seen our last human being for that day. Which is one great reason why I liked Juniper Creek. People are fine, but some days and some places are better without them. That applies to me too, in spades.

The water was shallow for the first hundred yards or so. You couldn't paddle. You drifted and poled along and made the turns by shoving at the banks with your paddle. But very soon the tiny brook swelled to double and triple its size, fed by the runoff from the springs called "The Aquarium." Now you could paddle if you wanted to. Or you could simply drift and steer if you preferred.

I never knew exactly what to do, for the stream worked subtly on my double-mindedness. On the one hand there was a tendency to linger because it was quieter without the dull thump of paddle shaft against boat; because there was no hurry; because the present spot was lovely beyond excelling and, once left behind, couldn't be re-lived until the next trip—and in this uncertain world, when would that be?

In this mood I asked myself, "When do you live, if not *now*?" and placed my paddle, dripping jewels, across the thwarts. I watched the soft play of light and shadow on the sand, the easy undulation of the underwater weeds, the fingerlings slowly cruising. I began to muse on deep and pleasant things—and who could help it, here on a stream of water where everything combined to evoke a stream of consciousness? Who could resist warm sunlight, gently dappled; great cypress, immovable in one spot for obvious centuries and quite content to be so; the patient relaxed droop of grey moss hanging from old limbs; the silent stream, everlasting symbol of man's unconscious, carrying one forward without effort—and all this wrapped in brooding stillness?

But then a startled lizard scuttled suddenly on the bank, and all at once I dipped my paddle strongly, eager to find out what was around the bend. In this new mood I wasn't content just to let the stream take me, but I had to put my own back into it. Everything around me was alive and seemed to call out the active response of my own life.

128

In some of this world's moods and places I have found sunlight that is joyless, and water that is sullen, and beauty that is cloying, and silence that oppresses. But not on Juniper Creek, even that day it rained. Here was lightness, sparkle, zest, and forward pull. And so I paddled briskly, hurrying down to the deeper, stronger, wider, water. To the deeper, wilder, forest.

Then, "Rig up my fishing pole, please!" I would call to my wife in the front seat. "I seem to remember that the first big pool isn't too far ahead now."

So she rigged while I paddled. And then she paddled while I fished. But fairly soon we drifted against the bank and decided that it was time to have a cold drink and a sandwich. The other mood had again descended, and we were happy just to sit and look and listen, yet quite content when the current decided to swing us away from the bank and carry us silently onward once more.

At the start of my first trip I had asked the ranger, "Is there any fishing in this stream?" By the question I had meant to inquire if fishing were legal in the game preserve through which Juniper flows.

"There's plenty of fish there," he said. Then he added with a smile, "If you know how to get 'em out." Thus he answered my question and left me with a new one.

I'm not the world's best fisherman although I've done my share of it in various places. Added to that, on Juniper Creek I didn't work very hard at fishing—somehow it seemed rather a waste of more important time. Oh, I was always telling myself that next trip, or the one after that, I'd definitely set aside as a fishing trip pure and simple. I never did, on the five trips we took, but someday maybe I will. Yet, spasmodic and most unscientific as I was about it, I never failed to catch fish, in highly satisfactory numbers. Indeed, on one trip we must have hit the solunar table exactly right because for the only time in my life I got tired of catching fish. (Note to game wardens: I have never brought a fish home from Juniper Creek. We put them all back as soon as we caught them.)

They weren't big ones—although I have seen some truly monstrous bass in Juniper, and a skin-diving friend of mine who went with goggles and fins down its lower reaches on a crabbing expedition brought back corroborating visual evidence. For the most part the fish I caught were a species of red-breasted bream, the largest being about the size of your hand. But they acted like rainbow trout, especially on that record day. They hit savagely, they dived deep and hard, they broke water, they flashed brilliant in the sun. No fishing, anywhere, could possibly have been more fun.

The bass, if possible, were even more alive. Even the tiniest of them proved that bass are born with complete knowledge of the entire bag of tricks. Even the six-inchers stood on their tails, savagely rattling their gills. Even these tiny ones plunged unerringly for the logs and snags or left me with slack line by coming straight at me or suddenly showed up on the wrong side of the boat, laughing as they broke free.

I have fished for dolphin and sail off Fort Lauderdale; for bass in New Hampshire and North Carolina lakes; for trout in the streams of Colorado and the mountains of Carolina; for sea trout in Mosquito Lagoon; for red bass in Spruce Creek; for the brisk schooling bass of Lake George and the heavy lunkers of the St. John's. Successfully, too. If I'm not careful, I'll start telling you about the time when, wading Lake George, I stood in one spot and on four successive casts caught a seven-, a five-, a four-, and a two-pounder in that order.

But I would as soon fish Juniper Creek as any place I know, even if the ones I've taken there have been small. To my mind fishing is relative anyway. Small fish on light tackle do as much for me as huge monsters on heavy stuff. Perhaps more, for various reasons. The physical surroundings of Juniper Creek cannot be excelled, to cite one.

When fishing Juniper I used a tiny creek rod, weighing about an ounce, which I originally acquired for use on the smaller trout streams of North Carolina. The only lure I bothered to use was a small Colorado spinner. Some day, I say again, I may really fish that stream, using everything I own. Then again, maybe I won't. I've done all right so far without it, for Juniper had other values for me besides fishing.

It will for you too, if you like to glide around a quiet bend and, ten feet away, scare the daylights out of a deer that is taking a drink. If you like to tingle to the heavy crash of what you suppose, possibly correctly, is a bear in the brush fifty feet away. If you like to watch squirrels scuttle sharply across the brittle leaves or to peer back at peering raccoons or to laugh at possums laboriously climbing. The bird life, too, is fantastic, but who can describe Florida's birds? The ponderous herons, the nervous ducks, the raucous woodpeckers, and the dozens of others that, in my ignorance, have no names?

I liked, too, the gigantic trees, collectively and in their occasionally weird individuality. The orchids growing wild and the cypress knees just standing there. A trained naturalist, passing through this untouched subtropical jungle, would undoubtedly go berserk in the profusion. Perhaps it's just as well that I am totally uneducated in this line and was content to take a general look across the forest floor as seen from the rabbit's point of view—exactly level with my eyes as I glided along.

And through it all wound the ever-changing river, like the stream of life ever deepening as the feeder streams continued to trickle in but, unlike life, remaining utterly clear. Clear, yet at the same time constantly changing color. Sometimes it glided, blue and green, beside a weed-grown bar. Sometimes it plunged, swift and black, between cut banks. A moment later, grey and lazy, it stopped completely for a while to create a long back-eddy in a shaded pool. Then it burst into the sun again, suddenly clear and colorless as air once more.

Should you be a good paddler and a good swimmer if you make the trip? Is Juniper Creek dangerous at all?

Not particularly. People have turned over in it, I am told. We almost did ourselves, once. There were three of us in the canoe that day, plus all our gear, and everybody was minding his own separate business when, on going 'round a bend, we slid sidewise underneath a fallen tree that angled up out of the stream bed. At once, three unorganized people started taking care of the situation in three separate manners, which is not a good idea in a canoe on fairly swift water. We made it safely, for no good reason.

However, if we hadn't we simply would have gotten wet. Oh, all of us could swim, including my seventy-year-old mother, who was the third passenger that day. But I think that even nonswimmers would be safe in Juniper Creek. The bank is never more than ten feet away, and the current would be bound to wash you there in a couple of seconds.

As a matter of fact, now that I write about this possibility, I think that the next time I take the trip I'll be sure to go swimming. On purpose. I know just the pool—a lovely hyacinth-bordered spot, complete with fallen tree, that ought to provide excellent fishing too. The temperature of the water is always perfect. I understand that it stays at about seventy degrees the year around.

It would help, I am sure, to know something about paddling a canoe, both for ease in coming around the bends, especially as the current strengthens, and also for getting through the last couple of miles.

Here, in its maturity, the whole character of Juniper Creek changes. The banks spread out until they are a hundred yards apart, or even more, and you find yourself in a hyacinth-choked river. There is no perceptible current now, so to get anywhere you have to supply your own power. Yes, it would help to know how to paddle.

In some ways those lower reaches are the most fascinating of all. The birds are more numerous and more plainly seen—you are out in the open. The fish, especially the skittish mullet, flee before you in greater legions. The purple hyacinth, that beautiful pest, is more abounding. The great dark coves cut into the banks are more mysterious. An old road comes out of nowhere, staggers on rotten piling across a man-made narrows, and goes nowhere. (My, the big fish that live in the deep hole under that old piling!)

Down in this area, in short, the whole scale is larger. You are on a genuine river that is a great deal like the St. John's, which is surely one of the most beautiful rivers in the world. And here a slight element of skill, or judgment, begins. If to make your wilderness adventures complete you have to have a bit of danger, preferably more imagined than real, this stretch will make your day.

You see, for eleven or twelve miles you simply followed a single unforking stream, without any possibility of getting lost. But now there are manifold channels through the hyacinth and other vegetation, and you have to take your choice. To make this more difficult, sometimes the rushes are higher than your head when you stand up in the canoe, so you can't see where in the world you are going. I forbear drawing obvious parallels to our course through life itself.

Somebody, at some time, erected stakes in the forks of the channel, with arrows pointing to the correct choice. Most of these arrows were still accurate in my day, but a few were missing even then—or the passing years had created new mazes—and at least one arrow pointed crazily to the sky. In running this minor labyrinth we made a few bad guesses every trip and came to a couple of dead ends each time. Sometimes, glimpsing the true channel lying clear and open over there, separated from us by only twenty feet or so of hyacinth, we fought our way through. But matted hyacinth is stubborn, inch-by-inch stuff, and if any great amount of it lay before us we chose to back out and try again. Of course, new markers may well be posted nowadays. I'll find out when I go back.

But it was different, mildly challenging, and sometimes rewarding to find new channels in those all-but-unmarked days. Indeed, it was on our third trip, when for the first time we tried to get through by hugging the left bank, that we discovered a heavenly spot we had never noticed before. A blue spring surged up, not much bigger than twice the size of your living room but making a perfect gem of a pool. On subsequent trips we always chose this way out, just to savor that place again.

My friend Andy's value judgment on the Juniper Creek canoe trip is as good as any I have heard. To appreciate Andy's appraisal for what it is fully worth, we will back up sixty days and get him in focus. He and his wife Mary took the Juniper Creek trip with my wife and me on the last day of a two-months' vacation jaunt. (Their jaunt, not ours. On a clergyman's stipend we can't go in for that sort of thing, any more than you. We just silently envy the people who can—occasionally vocalizing our bitter laments in loud tones, to be sure—exactly as you do.)

Their odyssey had taken them all over the Caribbean—Haiti, Puerto Rico, the Bahamas, the Virgin Islands—and South Florida. They had been deep-sea fishing, sailing, night-clubbing, skin-diving, mountain-climbing, swimming, exploring—oh, what would *you* do if you had sixty days and unlimited funds to spend in that geographical area? Well, that's exactly what *they* did.

On the last day of this junket, en route home, they visited us in Daytona Beach. Far into the night we listened, with considerable awe, to the account of their recent experiences. The next morning we took them on the Juniper Creek canoe trip. And at the end of it Andy was the one who was awed. He stood on the bridge, gazing back up the river, and said, "This has been the best day of our whole vacation."

After a while he turned to help me load the canoes on the tops of our cars. When we had that chore finished he said it again: "This is the best day of our whole vacation." I am quite confident that he really meant it, and his saying so brought great satisfaction. As you well know, it's often difficult, from a lean purse, to entertain and please your treasured friends as you would like to and as they deserve. If you are ever in that boat and also in central Florida, launch forth on Juniper Creek.

REALITIES DEEPEN

FOURTEEN

Clergy Wives

. . . we are left-handed people in a right-handed world.

I am deaf in one ear, so a deer has every advantage when I am stealthily stalking or just standing still waiting for one to come by. I can hear it rustling the dry leaves, but I haven't the least idea where it presently is or soon will be. With monaural hearing you can't even locate an airplane in a clear sky. It helps only a little to turn your head this way and that, like a radar scan, searching the direction from which the faint sounds seem to come loudest. You do much better if you take your wife along to be your ears on your blind side, if I may mix metaphors. When the leaves rustle, she will be looking in the correct direction. Keep your eyes on her and you will be properly oriented immediately.

The same holds true in the world of people. Let us postulate a social occasion when one detects a faint rustling in the leaves but cannot tell whence it comes or whither it goeth.

"Who in the world was that?" I mutter as I bestow a cucumber sandwich upon my spouse, having just disencumbered myself of an undesired and vaguely threatening presence.

"That was the notorious Harriet," I am instructed. "She eats clergymen for breakfast."

"So that was Harriet. Gave me the creeps."

"Could give you worse than that. Remember poor Jack?"

"She was the one? Well, I'll be darned."

"'Damned' is the word you're groping for."

"I hear you. Now who's that?" I indicate a faintly familiar face across the crowded room.

"That's the mayor's wife," I am told *sotto voce* and with the same unerring accuracy. "You've probably seen her picture in the paper. She's deeply concerned about dyslexia. She'll be coming to see you to explore the possibility of using the school's facilities during the summers. By the way, her name's Celia."

"How do you know these things?" I ask over my shoulder as I cross the crowded room. "Celia!" I exclaim. "So good to find you here. We have a lot to talk about."

A good case can be made for clerical celibacy, but don't look for me to make it. I have of course known dozens of splendid celibate clergy, male and female, in many denominations, but only they can truly testify to the freedoms and limitations, the opportunities and temptations, peculiar to their state. The same holds true with regard to married women clergy. I would have liked to title this essay "Clergy Spouses," but I know little or nothing about "The Clergy's Husbands," the contributions they may make to the ministries of their wives, or the way they feel in their roles. I know only one married couple both of whom are ordained—who, in fact, for some years were co-rectors of the same parish. Theirs must be a fascinating story, which someday they may tell. I wish they would, for the unique path they trod side by side may someday become a heavily traveled road. But I myself can pay tribute, and that inadequately, only to clergy wives, for my active ministry was spent in the era when holy orders were a male preserve.

Incidentally, Episcopalian objectors to the ordination of women did not deny that they could be ministers and executives. Everyone knew that women could minister supremely well, with rare empathy, great spiritual fruitfulness, and on a high level. (Most people realize, however inarticulately, that the central task of religion is the redemption of Evil—that in this work the operative force is Love— and that in the last analysis Love is a feminine mystery.) Everyone also knew that women could administer parishes and dioceses as easily and ably as they run convents, manage businesses, or govern states and nations. Objections, in the Episcopal Church, to conferring holy orders upon a woman were based solely on theological considerations: in the light of scripture and tradition, could she be a valid priest or a genuine bishop?

I—we—also lived in the era before a housing allowance replaced the parish's rectory as standard equipment. Clergy wives (one to a customer) then enjoyed a strange and amphibious calling to be half cloistered nun and half emancipated modern woman. To begin with, she had no home of her own—and women have a strong nesting instinct. In those days when rectories stood next door to the church, they were not so much homes as Grand Central Station anyway.

Their architecture was curious. They were made of glass. Their bathrooms were so situated that when one stepped out of the shower she frequently emerged *au naturel* in the midst of five strange young children playing "Go Fish" on the bedroom floor. The front doorbell, the back doorbell, and the telephone were interconnected so that they all rang at once. The lady at the front door had come over from the parish house for a pair of scissors and improved her time by testing the dining room table for dust. The wino at the back door had had the misfortune to run out of money precisely there, on his way from Miami to New York where an alleged job awaited him. The inquirer on the telephone had a wrong number; he wanted to know why in the hell somebody

139

hadn't been down to fix his heat pump. Fortunately, none of these intrusions had awakened Sister Gertrude, napping in the front bedroom in preparation for her little talk that afternoon to the ladies of the Altar Guild, followed by lemonade and goodies prepared by you know whom.

Yet on a limited budget this zoo had to look and feel like a home, even a haven. Its mistress had to be stylishly dressed. Her children had to appear to be angels, even during those impossible years when, like all children, including the Junior Warden's, and despite their souls having been washed in the waters of baptism, they are essentially devils. So a minister's wife had to be a good manager, a discerning disciplinarian, a peerless diplomat, and fast on her feet. She also was an excellent short-order cook, seamstress, upholsterer, painter, paper-hanger, interior decorator, and charwoman in the morning, and a deft concealer of calloused hands when she appeared as a gracious hostess, prepared to suffer fools gladly, while pouring tea in the afternoon. In a careless moment my wife was once apprehended in this unavoidable deceit. "Isn't it too bad that you aren't a lady," the other lady said.

The minister's wife also, and far more importantly, had to be a spiritual director and a contortionist at all times, for her primary calling is to keep her husband humble while giving his vocation constant priority, meanwhile being and evermore becoming her own real self. That is extremely nice work, if one can do it. In my observation most do, against long odds.

In so doing they are essential to the full effectiveness of a minister. We married clergy depend utterly upon them for many basic facts, and all nuances, about our parishioners. We learn from them such hidden things as who isn't speaking to whom, and why, and how that silliness might best be rectified. We are alerted about crumbling marriages, unrecognized saints, available teachers, lonely grandmothers—the whole range of need for understanding there, sympathy here, and a Dutch uncle talk over yonder. Certainly we might have discovered these things ourselves, given a few months' time, but a few months' time can be a disastrously expensive luxury.

Clergymen—I am still writing as of the days when all clergy were men—are "set apart." Indeed they are. At Christmas their friends can enjoy the festival in a truly Christian manner while they themselves have to be in church most of the day and are unseasonably weary when they finally get home to the eager family. They are tied up on weekends, unable because of their strange hours to join their comrades as they celebrate Saturday night in the red-blooded American way or to be one of a foursome with them on Sundays. While our compensations greatly outweigh these severe sacrifices— we don't even have to bother about getting a starting time on Mondays—the fact remains that we are left-handed people in a right-handed world.

So are our wives. Man and wife are one flesh; hence, what happens to the one must happen to the other. The wife is set apart too, usually without benefit of ordination. Like her husband she may resent, even resist, the fact a bit at the start. I do recall an occasion when a clergyman friend of mine, who had not taken a day off for weeks and had begun to hear about that around the rectory, finally became not only aware and contrite but actually determined. Late Sunday night, after the Young People's meeting, he told his spouse to prepare a picnic lunch for the whole family the next morning and to keep the children home from school then, for on that sacred day they were all going to the beach together, come what may. Early in the morning she did so, with great joy, while Father slipped down to the church just for a moment. The lunch was prepared, the children stayed home from school, and everyone settled down to wait just for a moment. Finally the children ate their picnic lunch around the kitchen table and were sent to school for its afternoon session. At two o'clock Father came home, looked around in puzzlement, and asked his wife, "Where are the kids? And why aren't you ready?"

Yes, clergy wives have indeed been heard to say, "I've never seriously considered divorce, but murder does occasionally appeal." However, if our personal experience is typical, if the whole cloth repeats our small sample pattern, we all come rather quickly to prefer life the way we live it. For while we indeed are set apart, nevertheless we are set apart together. Without any question we have a glorious opportunity to grow even closer together over the passing years. We happily serve the same God. We are involved in the same work, with the same people, under the same roof. Even if that roof doesn't belong to us, our experiences there are parallel, our purposes are identical, so our values inevitably merge.

I think that clergy wives realize and cherish the truth stated before: that they have been given a genuine and a special vocation. I more than suspect that, like my own wife, they all sense God standing close behind them, not only steering them toward wisdom but also giving them the strength to handle everything that comes their way. That they view the difficulties and hardships they have to tackle (which are many) as exercises for their souls' growth and, hence, as enablers for the better service of all the members of the Church.

I believe you will find these opinions amply documented throughout the pages of this opus. So I am content to restate and stress, here, that three-dimensional ministry is difficult, if not impossible, to a mere male who lives in his two-dimensional world; a world which, so to speak, he wanders while deaf in one ear and blind in one eye, out of contact with a lot that goes on and somewhat bewildered by the rest. He cannot hope to function completely with his partial equipment. But his wife, like all women, has uncanny antennae. She is sensitive to and knowledgeable about more things in heaven and earth than are dreamed of in her husband's masculine philosophy. A clergyman's wife fine-tunes her standard feminine equipment, filters out the essence of what she discerns, graciously effaces herself, and dedicates all to the glory of God by vastly enabling the ministry of her husband.

FIFTEEN

Descent into Hell

*. . . she led my whole family
down into the pit with her.*

My son, who at age sixteen vacillated between considering me totally incompetent and all wise, brought the girl, one of his classmates, to me. She wasn't merely shy, withdrawn, terrified, paranoid. She was on hard drugs. She was the first lost soul in that hell-on-earth—this was thirty years ago—that I had ever met. It took me more than a year of walking on eggs just to gain her wary confidence. After she finally began to talk, here a little and there a little, she led my whole family down into the pit with her.

I never met any of the pushers. I never heard a name nor saw a face. Yet obviously the mob was watching all the time, doubtless wondering how much I was beginning to know. Somewhere along the line they started to send calling cards.

My telephone began ringing every twenty minutes around the clock, with never so much as a breathing at the other end. After many such months a voice finally spoke. "We're going to kill you," it said, and the caller hung up. My son had answered the phone. From that time forward he did his homework with a loaded shotgun in his free hand. He was a very sick boy, awaiting his turn for open-heart surgery, at the time. I went to an unlisted number, telling only my Bishop and Senior Warden why. They understood and sympathized. My thousand parishioners did not.

The pressure increased. Outside my office door one morning I found a pool of blood, with five bullets arranged around it. My family, plus that girl, numbered five. From then on when I left the house in the morning, nobody was sure I'd ever be returning.

One night soon afterwards there came a knock on the door of our rectory. My daughter, home for the weekend from college, opened it. The battered, bruised, bloody, and unconscious girl—about whom we had never told our daughter—fell or was pushed out of the darkness into her arms. It took us quite a while to locate a doctor.

Shortly after the girl was able to leave the hospital, she brought me a sealed package, about the size of a shoe box. "It's got everything in it," she told me. "Names. Addresses. Occasions. The whole bit. Put it in your office safe. I'm going to the people and tell them you've got it, and that they'll have to stop pushing drugs and get out of town. I'll tell them that if they don't, or if anything happens to me, you'll take this evidence to the Feds."

I stared at the package lying on the desk between us. "No," I said. "We're amateurs. You and I are going to take this to the professionals, to the Feds, right now."

We argued, and I lost. The girl took the package and left. I went to the Feds alone and empty-handed. It was hard to tell from their poker faces whether they believed my story or not, but they said they would look into it.

I never saw nor directly heard from them again, but the mob soon went underground and the girl disappeared. A couple of years later we learned, quite by accident, that she had come up out of hell, cured of her addiction, and still walks this earth, breathing free. I can't vouch for this because I've never seen her again. I wouldn't know what she looks like now, and her name has gone from my mind. You can easily pray for nameless and faceless people.

Naturally I had to grapple with the drug scene again and again after that as the years of my ministry flowed by. There is no need to cite instances, no need to demonstrate that the drug culture (infelicitous combination of words) is one of our nation's, and of the world's, most vicious unsolved problems. Drugs probably ranks up there among the Top Ten Problems on any reader's list, along with such matters as global pollution of another sort. Along with mass starvation . . . terrorism . . . the threat of nuclear war . . . overpopulation . . . and so many other clear evidences of the collapse of culture as this dying century totters toward its close.

Surely every really civilized society must be marked by its honoring, by its providing a secure environment for, truth, beauty, and goodness; for creativity, freedom, and art; for adventure, harmony, and a vital peace. A more than civilized society, it is suggested in an old book, would be marked by the presence throughout it of such items as "love, joy, peace; longsuffering, gentleness, goodness; faith, meekness, temperance."

To come back to earth and the source of the preceding quotation, our world is, on the contrary, marked by the rampant presence of "hatred, variance . . . wrath, strife . . . murder . . . and such like." By frenzy, ugliness, and clamor, I would add. All in all we are living in the suburbs of hell, apparently teetering on the edge of that Black Hole.

My family has not enjoyed our personal brushes with the world's nastiness nor, for that matter, have I. But I do thank God, in a way, that He has let me descend a few steps into hell with Him, so He could point out to me the face of the enemy and show me a few of his ways, to the end that I should be able to identify him when I meet him again. As when the father of a family up the street commits suicide. Or when the child of a parishioner is killed. Or when the directors abscond and the bank fails, wiping out a life's savings. Or when aghast and startled parishioners come to tell how some horror attacked them in the midst of their daily lives as they were just going along minding their own business. (Hostages could tell us that such is one of the enemy's favorite tricks, as could any victim of a mugging. I had a parishioner who could do the same. It really shocked him to the core when another parishioner offered him ten thousand dollars under the table if he would only sign here—sign this construction permit—and then look the other way.)

To exercise effective priesthood in a fallen world we have to know the enemy from experience. We have to find and fight him first within ourselves—in our hearts and in our circumstances. Having truly looked him in the eye there, we will see the more clearly to discern him in society around us. Above all, we will then have resource to minister to his other victims. In short, hellish experiences, from which can proceed heavenly abilities, are essential in the shaping of a priest.

SIXTEEN

Economics

St. Joseph had missed it by fifty cents . . .

We were the more pleased that Mary and Andy valued the Juniper Creek experience narrated a few pages back because we clergy, characteristically and chronically of limited financial means, have too little opportunity and wherewithal to respond in kind to the favors our friends lavish upon us. We owe them so much but can repay them so little. Even if they do not expect equal recompense, which they don't, it definitely is more blessed to give than to receive. We crave our share of that blessedness.

A small part of the great economic gulf separating clergy and laity is of semantic origin. I understand that in the secular world one receives a salary, which I define as financial recompense for work one has done. On the other hand, a clergyman receives a stipend, which I interpret to mean sufficient financing to enable him to do his work. God's work, that is to say. There is a difference.

I hasten to say I would not have it otherwise, except that I wish everybody received a stipend and nobody got a salary. I fondly imagine that this arrangement would get horse and cart in proper alignment the world over, whereupon all manner of things would be well. Meanwhile, I remain of the conviction that it is a good thing clergy stipends are, typically, quite small. The arrangement works to keep our calling from becoming merely a profession.

In using that word I intend no offense to my admired doctor, lawyer, and other friends in the professions. I do mean, first of all, that a clergyman's kingdom is not of this world, but he himself is up over his knees in it and needs every assistance to keep from becoming completely mired down in it. Furthermore, he needs help in making sure that he does not merely profess faith in the reality and power of the other world but really believes in it. That is to say, he does if he is like me. I have, however, had the privilege of knowing many of the other kind—the unworldly and even the otherworldly sort—whom I shall shortly extol. But first, some clarifying statistics.

I have said that clergy stipends are, or at least were, not overly vast, and I can only illustrate by citing my own financial history. At the start I was supposed to receive $1200 a year, which I didn't; in actuality about $80 a month came in. A rectory was supplied, but not the expenses of its utilities nor a car allowance. In my final year, four decades later, I received $11,000, with rectory and the cost of its utilities. In between this Alpha and Omega the stipend climbed with "unperturbed pace, deliberate speed, majestic instancy," so you can figure out the average. I imagine that this was about par for the course at the time. We all managed. Our stipends enabled us to do the work, if precious little else.

They also helped us to become somewhat unworldly, and I am convinced that that is the name of the game. In short, economics functions in the molding of the clergy by leading not to an existence in genteel poverty for no good reason but to the glorious liberty of the otherworldly children of God. The small but adequate stipend is a mighty force aiding one to grow in faith and, thus, without hypocrisy to lead others along that essential path. The limited, but not limiting, stipend helps a priest to seek first, last, and always the Kingdom of God, in perhaps timid but ever-growing confidence that all other things will in their proper time and measure be added unto him.

I have known many such clergy, bishops among them, to my own great enrichment. I knew a bishop who cut his stipend—from ten thousand to eighty-five hundred dollars, if memory serves—when the diocesan budget would not balance unless the giving to missions were lowered, which he would not permit. I knew a priest—he had a wife at home and two children in college—who, when his parish that shall be nameless was about to founder during the Depression because it could not meet expenses, told his worried vestry that if they would just keep a roof on the rectory and coal in its cellar everything would be all right. They did, and it was.

In our modern era the number of utterly non-stipendiary clergy is astonishing and growing. I know one who supports himself by teaching and farming on weekdays and on weekends tends his human flock. He tithes himself in support of the mission and accepts nothing in the way of stipend or travel expense. I know a perpetual deacon who serves an entire diocese under the direction of his bishop, traveling thousands of miles each year without any financial recompense, buying his necessary business machines, mailing out his quarterly newsletters. This sort of thing may well be the wave, or at least a ripple, of the future.

The present brief essay does not attempt to investigate all or even many aspects of a thorny subject—like vestries which grind the faces of the poor; like a non-tithing laity—but limits itself to the minister and his so-necessary development in holy indifference to worldly reward of every kind. Even with such limitations, and within the limit of sheer finances, the questions do arise: "What of emergencies?"; "What of the changes and chances of this mortal life?"; "What about old age?" Here we enter the area of "fringe benefits," "affirmatively answered prayers," and "the widow's mite."

149

I remember the time when some disaster threatened the parish of which I was rector. I have forgotten the exact nature of the crisis. Whatever it was, it was imminent, and it sufficed. Furthermore, it was clear to me that if the parish succumbed my stipend would also, leaving me looking around our dinner table saying, "Whence shall we buy bread that these may eat?"

Let's say that the church had to have a new roof. In any case $478.50—back in the days when a dollar was a dollar and few were to be found—was needed immediately and was nowhere in sight. I signed the roofing contract, if that is what it was, and then started thinking, which is better than worrying. I bethought me that the parish was dedicated to St. Mary, whose husband was St. Joseph, who was a carpenter and hence presumably knowledgeable about and interested in domestic repairs. So I went over to the church, lit a candle at St. Joseph's shrine, told him our troubles, and went about other business. A few days later I received a totally unexpected check for $478. St. Joseph had missed it by fifty cents, on the down side, but his timing was superb.

I tried, or used, or cajoled, him a few years later in another emergency, when an estimated, and so budgeted, parish house repair was set at two thousand dollars but because of one thing and another climbed toward ten thousand, a truly horrendous sum. Again St. Joseph delivered, on the nose. Since then I have let him pretty much alone. He scares me. St. Joseph produces exactly what I ask, without any censoring. Most of the time these days I let my prayers be known only to God, Who is aware of the difference between needing and merely wanting and responds accordingly.

Often I hear from Him a thunderous "Thus saith the Lord . . . NO!" Occasionally the answer is "Yes, and I'm glad you asked." Some years ago a young parishioner, a married man with two children, came to me to discuss his longstanding and strongly felt call to the priesthood, together with its attendant financial impossibilities. I had learned that God loves impossibilities, but you may be sure we studied that young man and the situation at length and depth before I went to lay the matter before one of the parish's wealthy saints.

"How much would it cost?" she asked, after I had vouched for the man, his family, and his call.

"With what he has and what he can earn, five thousand dollars a year for three years," I told her.

"You come at a good time," she said. "I have a rule that whenever I spend anything on myself I give an equal amount to something worthwhile, and I've just returned from entertaining myself and some friends on a yachting trip. It cost five thousand dollars, so I've been looking around for a matching opportunity. Let me give you my check for that amount now, and I will instruct my lawyer to see that you receive an equal sum in each of the next two years, whether I'm alive or dead."

By the way, she made a good investment. I have kept tabs on that young priest, who is not young any more.

Perhaps above all in this general connection I remember the little old saint, one of the two holiest souls I have known, who at the time of a parish's direst financial need came to me and poured on my desk in pennies and nickels her entire worldly fortune of seventy-eight cents. I had been worried about what might happen if we failed to meet our huge obligations—what might happen to the parish and consequently to me and mine—but from the moment of that deserved rebuke I had no further concerns whatsoever. And, of course, it came to pass that everything turned out well.

It also came to pass, later, through this same penniless saint and a host of other good people, that when we ourselves were drowning in the depths of a financial sea, the waters were parted on the right hand and on the left and we passed over on dry land. That was the way it was; that is the way it is; and I prefer to say nothing further here in commentary on St. Teresa's dictum that if we take care of God's business He will take care of ours.

SEVENTEEN

Medicine

Our daughter, born in 1937, came at fifty dollars.

It seems to me, on looking back, that the science, art, and practice of medicine turned a corner during the 1930s, then shifted into high gear, and has been steadily accelerating ever since. The discovery of penicillin in 1929, the use of sulfa drugs as bactericides beginning in 1932, and a hundred other subsequent medical advances bolster this thesis, but I am really basing my layman's opinion on a lifetime of personal experience.

For example, when my tonsils and adenoids were extracted in the early twenties, the anesthetic was straight ether, and the process of going to sleep seemed dreadfully slow, if infinitely preferable to staying awake. Anesthetics had been improved upon in time for my appendectomy a decade later, but after the surgery I lived a life of languor, going about things gingerly, for quite a spell. Yet when my brother's turn for the same operation came along, only a few years later, he was swimming and diving within a very few days.

My most eye-opening personal experience with the advance of surgery during the past decades occurred when, a few months ago, I had a cataract-with-lens-implant operation. Back in the bad old days, if I remember correctly, the recuperating victim lay in bed for a couple of weeks with head immobilized between sandbags and afterwards wore glasses ground from the bottoms of classic Coca-Cola ·bottles. I don't know what the operation itself felt like at that time and don't wish to be informed, but today it is a piece of cake, surely harder on the surgeon than on the patient. My brief outpatient session was over almost before it began, and two days later I was driving my car, going about business pretty much as usual, but in a world emerged from the shadows and newly brilliant with color. Within a reasonable time I was also driving a golf ball. Before the operation, when life was lived in the twilight zone, even with glasses I had had no idea where my tee shot ended up. Now, without them, I know all too clearly. It's over there, across the river and into the trees. However, with my new bright eyes, usually I can find it, or another one sufficiently like it, within the canonical five minutes. The saving in lost balls adds up. Forty-two years from now I will have paid for the operation in this way alone.

Again: childhood diseases, that catch-all term for chicken pox, German measles, red measles (rubeola; the Real Thing), mumps, whooping cough, and croup, used to be spoken of as "par for the course," or even in terms of "get it and get it over with." Those ailments are all pretty much in the past now, joining diphtheria, which had begun to yield to science around the turn of the century. In my youth, however, a sure sign of spring was the red rash of warning quarantine signs that sprang up on front-porch pillars.

I didn't list scarlet fever among the mere childhood diseases because in my youth it was in the big leagues. My brother and I acquired it simultaneously at some time during World War I. They came for us, wrapped us in blankets against the winter cold, carried us outside to their ambulance, and took us away to a pest house somewhere, where memory says we were quarantined interminably.

154

As we convalesced, our parents were allowed to come and, standing in the snow outside the closed, barred windows, make signs to us conveying news of the outer world and intelligence as to what toy or game or cookie they had brought along. No, before penicillin scarlet fever was not an ordinary childhood disease. I think it was what made me deaf in my right ear.

The flu epidemic that was visited upon the suffering earth at the end of World War I was in that same category. Our family escaped it, having paid our dues via scarlet fever, but my wife's family didn't. She and her three brothers were all down with it at once, ministered to by their parents—doctors were desperately busy or were themselves dropping like flies, so that you couldn't get one for love nor money. My wife tells of her mother sitting on the foot of the sickbed, beginning to talk to her but falling asleep from utter exhaustion as she sat there.

A third big-league disease stalked us in the early 1950s. We were on vacation at the ranch when, one Saturday night after the square dance, Bill came to our cabin to say, "We've got trouble." The sudden illness of a child in the next cabin had been diagnosed as polio. All the children, ours included, had been on a picnic together that noon. While they were homeward bound, the rains came, and they all huddled together under a blanket in the back of the truck, damply breathing on each other for a soggy hour or so. A perfect atmosphere for passing polio around, one would think—and some of us did think.

The polio epidemic closed our city down—no movies, no church services, no public gatherings of any kind—and quarantined us out at the ranch for the duration. The days passed slowly at first, but as time went by the sick youngster's case proved to be a mild one, and nobody else got the disease. From then on, ours was not a fate worse than death, for the ranch would be back in business and, meanwhile, Bill's horses had to be exercised daily. Jonas Salk would come to the world's rescue almost immediately afterwards.

Before discussing pre-1930s household pharmacopeia, let's be sure to distinguish between childhood diseases and the occupational

hazards of childhood. By occupational hazards I mean, in no particular order of chronology, frequency, or severity, such things as: the
stubbed toe, the black eye, the burn, the blister (water and/or
blood), the skinned knee, the strawberry, the broken arm, the
bruise, the charley-horse, the torn ligament, the frozen finger, toe,
and ear, the bee sting, the sprained ankle, the scratch, the gash,
and the laceration. These things are still with us and always will be.

We can also at this point dismiss, again in a very few words, the
environmental health hazards aspect of our study-in-depth. Before
the 1930s there was a general awareness and acceptance of a malev-
olent streak running through this fallen world: i.e., the existence of
copperheads, of weak branches on tall trees, of vines cunningly
hidden to trip you up, of cozy hearth-fires that suddenly flared and
set you ablaze. Aside from these aspects of the problem of evil,
however, the only recognized environmental health hazard of my
youth was the ledge of rock in the middle of our high school's
football field. As time went by, the school administration took care
of that, leaving us only at the mercy, or whim, of acts of God. It was
widely believed that this was the way things ought to be.

To get back on the main track, I record that preventive medicines, pre-1930, were three in number: (1) Father John's, a tonic
which looked and tasted brown. Its ingestion immediately induced
upchucking in sensitive victims like my sister, so its long-term
benefits to her and her ilk were dubious; (2) cod-liver oil, which it
was thought that I imbibed daily for years. In truth, I actually did
gag down dozens of teaspoons of the dread and horrible stuff, which
I believe was supposed to be full of vitamins and awfully good for
you. In time, however, I weakened (or strengthened) and began
anointing the head with oil. Our john became richly fortified, if
cod-liver oil is indeed all they claim for it; (3) Lydia Pinkham's,
which I never understood.

Curative, or remedial, medicines came in greater variety, but no
abundance. There was peroxide, the mild fizzy antiseptic of choice
for lesser abrasions. Then there was iodine for the deeply lacerated
and the brave. Sucking in your breath through pursed lips and

clenched teeth, you put this on the hurt place. The iodine burnt like fire, so obviously it was killing germs by the million.

Witch hazel, cool and soothing and cleansing, could be used on bites, bee stings, and everyday contusions to make you feel better, I am told. I'm not sure I ever tried it. Mostly I managed to be bitten and stung when far from home, where mud was the analgesic ready to hand.

I approach the subject of castor oil with reluctance. It was a concoction horribly dreadful beyond belief. All sorts of ingenuity were expended on attempts to disguise its taste, but none was successful or even mitigating. Castor oil conquered all. The best you could do with it was hold your nose, close your eyes, and be resolute. If your imagination, your psyche, or your physical innards revolted and sent it back up again, there was more where that came from and a parent was standing firmly by. Vigilance was strict, so I was never able to determine whether castor oil would unstop a sink. I'm sure that my parents had been there before me, in their own younger days, and knew all the tricks.

Boric acid was for eye-wash during pinkeye and conjunctivitis. Epsom salt dissolved in hot water was for soaking sprains and infected sores; in a poultice it served for drawing boils. I *think* we also used poultices of laundry soap—good old Octagon—perhaps mixed with sugar, and that this worked like a charm, but my memory is foggy on the point and the other gaffers whom I've queried on the subject during my research are no help. They frown at me and sternly say they don't recall any such thing. Although I've reached the age of wisdom, by which I mean that I'm not dog-matically certain about anything any more, I stick to my minority opinion, possibly delusion, on this subject. I prefer to think that my elderly friends have lost their minds entirely or just never had boils when young. I did.

Rolls of gauze for use as bandages did exist, but almost everybody hunted up an old bed sheet, tore in into strips, and tied it in place, where it would often stay for a while. It's a severe reflection on our brains that we never thought of inventing the Band-Aid. We certainly had enough opportunity and motivation.

An essential surgical instrument was to be found in the sewing cabinet, not the medicine chest—a needle with which, after disinfection by holding it in a flame, you extracted splinters.

Some homes, including ours, kept a further and final medicine—whiskey or brandy—hidden away in a closet to be available in case of pneumonia. We ourselves credit mustard plasters fore and aft, plus warmed brandy administered with an eye-dropper forced between rigid lips, for saving our baby daughter's life at one dreadful time during the late 1930s.

Even as early as the 1920s in our town, several doctors had joined forces to practice group medicine, which I thought was an excellent idea. For the most part, however, a doctor then practiced solo, and in many cases his office was in his home. Ours was of this sort, and especially that time I was long-jumping while somebody was using a spading fork at the other end of the pit, I'm glad he was. When I hit one of the fork's tines with my face, I knew that our doctor was just around the corner from the school where the accident occurred. Naturally he was an old friend, too. He'd been in our house a dozen times, as was the custom in those days.

"Where have you been?" he greeted me. "I haven't seen you for a couple of weeks. Now let's see what you've got here."

After he patched me up he probably gave me a gumdrop to sustain me on my long trip home, but I've forgotten as to that. In any case, the family doctor was a great institution that I'm glad to see is coming back. To say this is in no way to denigrate the hospital emergency room, with all its specialized staff and equipment. I learned this even back in the twenties, when we took my brother to the hospital after he had fallen thirty feet out of a tree, breaking himself all to pieces. The work the emergency team did on him was almost magical.

Professional medicine didn't cost all that much in those early days, before Medicare, before the malpractice suit had really caught on, before all that expensive new equipment, before the dollar lost most of its value. My medical insurance, back then, paid an adequate six dollars a day for a hospital room. Our daughter, born in 1937, came at fifty dollars. I'm not in a position to know the price of daughters now, but I imagine it's more than that. Our son, born in 1940, cost about the same figure with all his original equipment, but unfortunately some of that was faulty. With him we entered the era of really modern medicine, with its escalating expertise and rapidly rising expense.

When our son was born with his septal defect, the only useful thing they could teach medical students on that subject was how to tell the parents that their child would not live long. Any surgeon could have sewed up the hole between the ventricles; the baffling trick was to get inside the heart to do so, while keeping the patient alive. Seventeen years later this doomed child had successful open-heart surgery. Even then the odds against him and his fellows were ominous—fifty-fifty or worse—but he had reached the point, after four massive heart failures, that it was one hundred to one he'd die within the year if he refused the available operation.

"I don't want to go to the hospital next fall," he told our doctor, who was urging the operation. "I want to go to college then."

"Son, without the operation you won't ever go to college," the doctor said.

Our son elected to put college off for a year, and thus we plunged into the new medical world. "There will be a deposit of fifteen hundred dollars," the receptionist said as we signed on the dotted line at a famous hospital, one of the very few at which the work was then being done. A month and many thousands of dollars later his mother and I had the privilege of looking at him in the recovery room.

I have never seen another human being so wired and tubed. That unconscious kid was the pulsing center of a vibrant machine. From every natural opening in his body, plus a dozen more made with skillful knives, connections ran to dials and gauges on the wall.

He was remote and silent in the farthest loneliness, but he hid no secrets; the nurses and doctors read him loud and clear.

My wife and I spent a lot of time in that hospital, going down to hell and back and trying to comfort others on the same journey. The place was a world center for research and treatment; we met people who had come there from Australia and Zanzibar. They arrived from the antipodes via luxury liner and jet plane; they established their beloved securely within the hospital's walls; and then they looked around for a place where they themselves could stay while the medical wheels ground exceeding fine and exceeding slow. Those who had come the greatest distance—around the actual Cape of Good Hope—found themselves in a bad case, merely because they had left their automobiles at home. They were forced to stay within walking distance of the hospital.

My wife and I had inspected those available hovels with some thought of taking one and with mounting gratitude that we had been able to drive our seventeen hundred miles and were free to select a good motel only thirty minutes distant. The enforced walkers had to settle for lumpy cots in the cubicles and curtain-partitioned hallways of grimy tenements. They had to stand in line with a dozen others outside the single bathroom each morning, or perform their ablutions in leisured splendor at midnight. We came to know a resourceful couple who borrowed pillows from the hospital storeroom and clandestinely slept in a broom closet there. Other facilities, with hot and cold running water, were just around the corner. They may now be telling humorous tales about "Thirty Nights in a Broom Closet," but it wasn't funny at the time when they were discovering the hard way just how far science had outstripped the rest of the humanities.

Nobody faulted the hospital then, and I'm not doing so now. Those doctors—ours was a team of seventeen—can have our right arms, up to here, for any good reason at any time. I merely wondered, then, why other human engineers hadn't realized that few people would ever come to that hospital unaccompanied—they wouldn't have the strength to make it alone—and that the company would need living quarters for a protracted and traumatic spell. That hospital was a splendid symbol of our technology; but in our day you couldn't live in it or, decently, anywhere near it.

I rejoice that there's been vast progress in this line too since those pioneer times more than twenty-five years ago; today there are many hospitals with guest rooms just around the corner from the surgical wing. Medicine and its allied arts are zipping along in a way to put a new heart, a new hope, into you every day. I'm delighted, medically speaking, that I and mine came along when we did, and not a minute sooner. For, I say again in a triumphant voice, our boy not only survived but is perfectly well and has a heart as sound as a dollar—if you will pardon that quaint and archaic expression.

EIGHTEEN

Telepathy

We chatted pleasantly at the door after service,
saying nothing in the usual ways.

I am not psychic, or mystic, or whatever the word is that they're misusing these days. I am not even particularly "aware" of situations and atmospheres. My best friends and worst enemies have often berated me for actions or remarks that, they say, even the social instincts of a half-awake congenital idiot would have avoided. Yet from time to time, inexplicably, I know things that are separated from me by great distances of time and space.

Like the time, back in my early ministry, when I was enjoying breakfast with my wife after an early Eucharist and an inner compulsion came strong and clear, saying to me almost in so many words— "Go to the hospital."

I glanced at my watch; the time was not yet eight o'clock. No self-respecting parish priest with any experience visits a metropolitan hospital at that hour. In my imagination I could see the nurses' lips tightening as I intruded my round collar into their early routine.

The compulsion was insistent. "John Stevens in the hospital."

"Now look here," I silently argued, "I saw John only yesterday, and he didn't seem too ill. A sick young man, without any doubt, but doing as well as can be expected. Wouldn't it be all right to wait until the usual time this afternoon before—"

"The hospital. At once."

Within ten minutes I was in John's hospital room. Two minutes later John was dead.

I had been able to give him the last rites and compose his body in death. It was I who called the nurses into his room—lacking my presence, John would certainly have died unnoticed, perhaps to lie in the quiet lonely room for some time. It was I who drove to his mother's home, which I reached before the official telephone call, reached, in fact, even as Mrs. Stevens was coming down the front steps to start her trip to the hospital. There was shock, but there was some comfort, too, when I was able to say, "I was with him when he died." The thought has not left me yet—suppose she had walked unprepared into that room downtown, with her bright expectant smile on her face?

The uncanny telepathic warning at the breakfast table is only one of dozens of similar experiences in my life as a clergyman. In fact, I think I went to the hospital against all the rules of common sense because over the years I have learned to trust the inner voice. It has never been wrong.

When it all started I do not remember. However, the first incident that I can recall clearly occurred about forty years ago, when I was a relatively immature priest. I was writing a sermon in midmorning when I was absolutely forced to stop all work and go at once to the home of a certain parishioner. There was no psychological reason for the urge; at least, none that I have ever been able to discover. The family in question had been at church the previous Sunday; everyone was well; we had chatted pleasantly at the door after service, saying nothing in the usual ways. Nevertheless, I left

164

the sermon half-written—my friends will tell you that this is a distinct sign of grace, as I am likely to swell up like a frustrated toad if interrupted in the midst of what I like to call a train of thought— and went to the designated house.

I'm sorry I can't tell you what I found there. You will simply have to believe me when I say that the unheralded visit possibly saved a life, probably preserved a sanity, and undoubtedly helped perpetuate a happy marriage. Furthermore, the timing was of the essence of the thing, as the lawyers say. The call had to be made exactly when it was made or untold harm might have followed.

From that time, similar telepathic urgings (let's call them that for simplicity) have come to me with fair frequency, perhaps one every couple of months or so. Since obedience to the prompting has invariably served me—and others—well, I have on occasion deliberately sought the queer guidance. Once, at least, this seeking was rewarded with success. I was idly driving through the city streets with no pressing business on my mind. The afternoon's work was done, but time remained to make another parochial call or two.

"Where shall I go? Whom shall I see?" I said to myself, invoking the genie of the lamp.

"Go to the Johnsons' home," he replied almost immediately, certainly before I had driven half a block.

I had been to the Johnsons' only a few weeks before. In the normal course of events I should not have called upon them for a few weeks more. They were good, quiet, elderly people, entirely faithful to the parish—and therefore the farthest folk from my thoughts because in this wicked world your priest is generally out looking into trouble-spots. He only visits the Johnsons when he needs his own faith, hope, and charity bolstered.

Yet I drove to the house, arriving simultaneously with the ambulance that had come for Mrs. Johnson. Her husband, poor broken-up old fellow, had been trying to get me on the telephone for an hour. I have always wondered if my telepathic instincts would have worked that day even if I had not tried to stir them up.

I have wondered, too, why the urges are so selective. For what they do warn me about I am thankful, but why do they skip over other occasions when I should be most grateful for their help? (Could it be I who tune them out?) They leave most of my emergencies untouched, which at times causes me no little annoyance with them. If the genie so often makes unnecessary the use of ordinary means of communication, why doesn't he put the Post Office, Ma Bell, and Western Union out of business altogether? They're not doing all that well as it is, so a simple shove might put them flat on their backs.

From what I have written it would seem that these visitations are always connected with tragedy or near-tragedy. That is true. The genie does not trouble himself to herald happy occasions. Perhaps this is just as well because of course one of the great elements of happiness is the very unexpectedness with which it happens. Therefore, on that score, I shall not trouble the spirit. Besides, perhaps there are great theological and philosophical implications latent in this fact. If we are warned only of catastrophe, then it may be that we have one more indication that evil is contrary to the real nature of things; that there is a force outside of nature making for good. In any case, if my inner spirit does not forewarn me of coming joy, I am content to have it so. Let the occasion surprise me unheralded and therefore be all the more joyful.

The foregoing account would make it appear that my promptings come only at precise split-seconds; that they tell of events separated only by space but never by time. In the main this is indeed the case. Certainly most of the evidence supports that conclusion. Yet there is another set of facts that may tell in the other direction.

A parish of which I was rector some years ago owned an island in Lake Winnipesaukee and made the island with its furnished cottage available for the use of the rector. For several years, in the heat of the summer, I would hie me to this cool retreat for a month or six weeks of ideal vacationing, punctuated by having the parish's young people come up for a couple of weeks of church camp. To make my life as pleasant and easy as possible there, I bought a few articles—hammock, outboard motor, pillows, books—which I left on the island each summer when I returned to the city.

Then there came a summer when I could not leave those personal articles behind. Something within me said—"You will not be returning to this place again. Take what is thine own, and depart in peace." It was a foolish thought, an absolutely senseless premonition. The island was not going to blow up or fly away, and certainly I was going to be rector of the parish until my (or its) dying day, for what other parish would take me—or, indeed, what other parish would I take? So I sneered at the genie the while I was obediently loading all my personal paraphernalia into my car.

I hardly need to say that the prompting was correct. The following spring I left that parish. I have never seen the lake or the island again, for now it is a perquisite of my successor, or perhaps it has been sold.

My wife could do a far better job on this subject than I can. She's much more "psychic," or "telepathic," or "sensitive," than I. Women, in general, are more so than men, I think. However that may be, she has on innumerable occasions become uneasily and vividly aware of situations looming in the lives of others remote from us geographically but close emotionally: like members of our family; or our circle of friends; or the boys at the boarding school where I was headmaster.

The most startling of these incidents occurred when she and I were at the General Convention of our Church in Louisville. On one of the evenings we were attending a special session to listen to a hot debate on the ordination of women. My wife and I sat up in the stands with hundreds of others, looking down at the speakers' tables just below us on the floor of the great arena. I imagine that most of us had our minds made up on the issue before the debate even began, but we gave it our close attention anyway, if only to find weak arguments to shoot down. My wife, it seemed to me, was particularly absorbed.

167

As soon as we were back in our hotel room after that session, she said, "Something has happened. We'll have to go back to the school."

I looked my questions.

"During that debate I saw some of the boys from our football team," she told me. "Down there just in front of the speakers' table, facing us. Four boys"—she named them—"standing there in their football uniforms . . . in a row . . . holding their helmets in their hands, looking at us. I saw them clearly. Something terrible has happened to them. We will have to go back to the school."

I hadn't seen them. I had seen only the arena, the spectators, the speakers. But I spent an uneasy night, for I recalled dozens of times when friend wife had been correctly alert to vibrations. I even remembered the time when we were living in Newark, New Jersey, and knew that old friends were then visiting New York City, but not the name of the hotel where they were staying. "Let's get in touch with them," my wife said. "They're at the Hotel New Yorker."

"New York crawls with hotels," I reminded her. "Why do you pick that particular needle out of the whole haystack?"

"Call the New Yorker," she said with great patience. "They're there." And they were.

Our school chaplain telephoned us in Louisville the next morning. The four boys my wife had seen—outstanding boys, all of them, leaders at the school, leaders-to-be in society afterwards—had slipped away from our school that night and driven home to South Carolina for a brief lark. On the return trip, in the small hours, the driver had fallen asleep at the wheel, totally wrecking their car. Two of the boys were unhurt. Another was horribly injured and hospitalized. The fourth, the driver, had been killed.

Those are the facts. I don't have any theories.

NINETEEN

Bigger and Better

*. . . we skate swiftly, if sometimes brilliantly,
over the thin and cracking ice. . . .*

On the Last Great Day, when I stand before the Judgment Seat to
hear the question that I am certain the Good Shepherd asks all of
His priests, "Did you feed my sheep?", I am going to have to drop
my eyes and mumble, "Lord, I never even knew them. They were
too many."

It is small comfort now, and will be smaller comfort then, that
legions of other clergy are in my miserable company. Indeed, it is
small comfort that countless pastors are probably worse off than I in
this regard, for mine were far from being the world's largest parishes.
The biggest one varied in size from six hundred communicants to
thirteen hundred, depending on the season of the year in that
tourist town.

Yet if my soul still troubles me because of my dealings—or,
rather, because of my lack of dealings—with this number of people,

how much more are some of my brother clergy being tormented. Perhaps I may speak for some of them. Certainly I shall speak *about* some of them, to help establish the situation of which I now write.

The first who comes to mind is my cousin, rector of a parish of eight hundred souls, who once told me of the seventy-seven candidates he had presented for confirmation the previous year. "I can't even tell you the names of more than a dozen of them now," he said. The names. The mere names. Remembering names was rendered impossible because of parochial size. Surely, then, any close pastoral relationship between priest and people was completely ruled out. The rector of a large congregation cannot even "get around" his parish in two years, unless he can run much faster than I could.

I think also of the lament of the priest, soon to be elected bishop but at the time rector of a parish of 950, when he was speaking about his Good Friday addresses of the former year. Because of the pressures that his great parish put on his time, he had not been able, with the best intentions in the world, to get at the necessary preparations. "I hate to think back on what I must have said," he told me. "And on Good Friday."

A priest out in California—now dead of a heart attack—wrote me that "about ten thousand new people move into this city each year, and five thousand move out. We do our best, but we only scratch the surface, if we do that. For my own soul's sake I've been trying for years to resign, but so far they've talked me out of it. Perhaps after we get the new church built, I can think about a smaller, more manageable work. Pray for me. I've never been so low."

But specific reference to dozens of other priests and a few bishops with whom I have talked on this subject of parochial size and its attendant subtopics can be omitted. I shall simply record that all of them felt alike on the subject. All of them stated that a parish which exceeds five hundred communicants has moved across the line which separates a family from a mob. All of them felt that in a parish of fewer than five hundred souls, the parish priest can know each person and each family with some degree of real intimacy, and vice versa. When Susan is getting ready to go to college, the rector knows it and is probably in on the discussions; indeed, Susan has undoubtedly sought his advice and counsel. When Johnny has his tonsils out, the priest is as emotionally and prayerfully aware of it as any other member of the family. But when the arbitrary number—five hundred—is exceeded, the law of diminishing returns sets in with a vengeance.

Incidentally, my only disagreement with this consensus is that the number five hundred is too high. In my experience, the two parishes that were most homogeneous, vital, and satisfying to everybody concerned were composed of 400 and 250 communicants, respectively (not "communicants" on paper in the parish roster, but real live ones existing in fact on Sundays and other days). But rather than haggle about exact figures and rather than get into the problem of the parish that is too *small* for real efficiency—an alien word in the context, but there it is—let's see some of the ways in which the law of diminishing returns does set in, both for priest and for parishioner, in the too-large group.

A good starting point is the fact of the physical and emotional breakdown of so many clergymen of our time—their brownout: the collapse of their priesthood. Breakdown among the clergy, an epidemic disease, can be traced to the burden of too much work in too many diverse fields. We—I believe I can still say "we" because the experience is still fresh, so from here on for a while I will—we must often, of necessity, skate swiftly, if sometimes brilliantly, over the thin and cracking ice of our manifold responsibilities. We all tried to be in two and sometimes three places at the same time, by breathlessly rushing from desk to hospital to schoolroom to board meeting. Somehow we got it all done, whatever "it" may be. But underneath in each ministerial heart there is the craving to be a real pastor, to penetrate below the surface. That is essentially why we are in the vocation. And since we cannot really express this chief drive in the large parish, we begin to cultivate a nasty group of frustrations, guilts, and even fears.

Added to enforced surface living is enforced living in an extensive sense while each pastoral soul among us craves intensive contact. It was C. S. Lewis who wrote that he didn't "see any sense in knowing more people than he can know well." Surely we are all haunted by the Gospel ideal of searching out the lost sheep until we find it. But in the large congregation we cannot. At the very best we can touch that sheep with the outer fringes of an organization, breathe a hasty prayer, and hope for the best. More usually, if my own experience is typical, we have to give up the hunt altogether, trusting that we can bury the memory of that soul in the limbo of forgotten things. Of course this is impossible, so two souls are now in danger, with the priest's being the first of them. He knows it, and the knowledge does not make his nights more restful.

Another item we lament is the fact that the large parish, with its attendant responsibilities, leaves us no time to read. The time that the clergy spend in study—or rather, do not spend in study—seems to come up at every session of the College of Preachers, every clericus meeting, every serious gathering of the clan.

This particular frustration goes far deeper. *Time* is required if a person is to ruminate, to think, to gestate, to soak, to mull, to pray. *Quiet* is also required for these essential exercises. And quiet is not simply the absence of noise and interruptions, but involves peace at the nerve ends, peace in the blood pressure, peace in the center of one's being. In peace and in quiet and in time the still small voice is heard. But this sort of quiet is what we cannot have in a large parish. Therefore we do not often, if we ever do, hear the sound of gentle stillness. Thus again we lose our souls—and know it.

As I have said before, the pressure of extensive duties creates a vacuum in our preaching—we don't know our people; we can't read, pray, or think; and as a result we can't preach. A rector admitted for all of us the other day that he hasn't preached a new sermon in a decade (that he stopped growing ten years ago?). "I've got the whole barrel catalogued and cross-indexed," he said. "Twentieth Sunday after Pentecost. Third Sunday in Lent. Patronal Festival. Worship—they're all at my fingertips. Usually I rearrange the paragraphs a bit, and if there's time I select new illustrations. I wonder if I'm fooling anybody. I do know *one* person I'm not fooling."

Our situation is akin to what the psychologists and sociologists term "alienation." For example, Eric Fromm in his work *The Sane Society* has some pages on the "process of quantification" and "the process of abstractification" which have been going on to the point that modern man (the term itself is an abstractification) has become "alienated." Estranged from himself. As out of touch with himself as he is out of touch with other people. All because he is out of touch with concrete reality on a man-sized scale. According to Fromm, we are all so alienated that we are just a short step away from needing an alienist.

His analysis culminates, for me, in his discussion of "bureaucratification." "Bureaucrats," he writes, "are specialists in the administration of things and of men. Due to the bigness of the apparatus to be administered, and the resulting abstractification, the bureaucrats' relationship to the people is one of complete alienation. They, the people to be administered, are objects whom the bureaucrats consider neither with love nor with hate, but completely impersonally."

And so it turns out that for many years, when in large parishes, I was not a parish priest but a bureaucrat. Well, I suspected as much for a long time, and so did my people.

Yet in all honesty I believe that the cause lay not in myself so much as in the sheer size of the operation in which I was involved. The law of size operated behind my back and made me do things in the bureaucrat's way, without giving me the freedom to decide whether the minister's way might be better.

I tried hard—we all try hard—to fight the law. In the attempt to increase pastoral effectiveness, the clergy employ 101 devices of tremendous scope and versatility, ranging from a Family Sunday to an anniversary Eucharist; from a Parish Life Conference to a personal letter; from a parish picnic to a telephone call; from a Vestry Retreat to a monthly newsletter to a grateful smile.

173

One scheme that is being used in the management of large-sized parishes is the parish administrator. I don't know anything about the idea from personal experience in practice, so I write subject to correction from those who do. (If a parish administrator friend of mine here in this town and/or another on Long Island happens to read this, I am going to get a letter, perhaps a phone call.) In theory, however, I should incline to be a little leery of the idea—not on the basis of possible personality clashes in the attempt to work out who is boss (we should assume that the parties involved would be Christians of a considerable degree of advancement in grace) but on the grounds that the problem of bureaucracy is not solved by creating another bureaucrat.

In the boom areas of the United States our parishes are not simply too large but are also growing too rapidly. Any living body can grow too furiously fast for its own health. In order for a parish to be itself, a living homogeneous contributing part of the Body of Christ, time is required. In order for people really to become part of the parish, time is required. But this time is bypassed in our great boom areas, where one mission is planted instead of two or three. All of us know dozens of spots where a mission was begun five years ago but which is at this moment a still-growing parish of six or seven hundred communicants, all of them somewhat lost. The single mission does not have to keep on growing unmanageably. A simple help would be the creation of another mission.

Long ago Aristotle pointed out that a city numbering more than five or six thousand heads of households was unfit for human life because it was out of scale. In our day, industry is learning that a group of something like one hundred families is the workable maximum for sanity, productivity, and happiness. It is my firm conviction that *all* groups have to be proportioned to the small stature of the human being.

We ought to prevent parishes from growing much beyond four hundred communicants. When one exceeds this size, the parish should forthwith start a mission. In order to enforce this as a law, at least three prime requisites would be necessary: (1) better standards of financial giving on the part of the laity; (2) higher levels of lay participation in the work of the parish; and (3) ridding ourselves of the slogan "Bigger and Better."

TYING TOGETHER

TWENTY

Weddings

Play it again, Sam?

Weddings are fun—solemn fun—but at the same time they are traumatic. So are the marriages they initiate. As the book says, they are "for better, for worse," which means in one interpretation that marriage is a dynamic union which, if it does not make a couple better, will inevitably make them worse. But let's stay with weddings, where all that begins. I repeat that they are occasions of solemn joy—of starry eyes on the part of young participants, admixed with some trepidation in the hearts of their battle-scarred elders. Smiling through one's tears at a wedding is almost an unavoidable phenomenon, certainly an entirely proper outward and visible sign. We do cry in our joys and also in our fears. (Be it said that, typically, brides do not cry. There are exceptions, but usually brides are as cool as cucumbers, utterly in command. The typical groom does not cry either, but for a different reason. He is benumbed.)

179

The trauma, the strains, of a wedding visit everyone closely involved; they fall upon the just and the unjust alike. Hence it is that a bottle of smelling salts, prominently positioned ready to hand, is standard equipment in every well-appointed sacristy and bride's room. Another way of expressing this same truth is to say that one of the blessings of retirement from the active parish ministry is consequent retirement from officiating at large weddings. Old and worn nervous systems are not up to that any more. We can still handle and greatly savor small intimate nuptials. The simple sacrament of holy matrimony is one thing and remains within our powers. A large society wedding can be quite another matter, far beyond our strength. In the mercy of God and the providing of canon law those affairs fall to the lot of our youngers and betters, of clergy still with good muscle tone and nerves of steel.

For the clergyman, be he just or unjust, is always close to the heart of the maelstrom, experiencing at least some of its buffeting winds. Let me illustrate by citing an occasion in my early ministry when the bride clearly bore the brunt—a wedding when the groom failed to appear at the stated time and place.

He existed, beyond doubt. He had attended the rehearsal and all the other preliminary rites, but he was forty minutes late in showing up for the main event. His cool calm, when finally he sauntered in, amazed me. I expressed my amazement to him in some words which I am confident his bride improved upon later, but at the moment she was speechless. Speech does not flow fluently when you are being revived with smelling salts, when you are choking and gagging.

This contretemps occurred some forty years ago but remains fresh in my memory. Because of it, I evermore changed my groundrules in regard to grooms, explaining nicely but firmly why they must present themselves to me not later than fifteen minutes before the appointed time. And because of it I always had a female attendant, preferably a wife, standing by to administer restoratives if and when needed.

I was strongly reminded of that experience some twenty years later when the mother of the bride—a subsidiary player when compared to a groom, to be sure, but nevertheless in an important cameo role—failed to arrive at the church on schedule. For some reason I forget, or never knew, the wedding of her daughter was being held in a city strange to Momma, who elected to stay in a motel some miles from the church. Momma made it to the rehearsal, of course, thus in my fond opinion locating the scene of the next day's action. Overnight, unfortunately, she not only forgot the church's whereabouts but also its name and mine along with it. As the appointed hour drew near, there was no way she could get in touch with me or even with her daughter, who was dressing in our anonymous church's bridal room.

Lacking the mother of the bride, a wedding does not start. The lady is the last one in, escorted by the head usher, who then pushes the button that triggers a light in the sacristy and on the organ console, whereupon all manner of things are set in motion. Until an organist sees the light he simply keeps on playing around (which is spiritually true of all of us, to be sure). My organist—his name really was Sam—did so. Interminably.

Some twenty minutes after the appointed nuptial hour Sam erupted from his organ bench into the adjoining sacristy to announce that he had run through his entire repertoire twice and now what should he do?

"Play it again, Sam," I told him.

Not too cheerfully Sam did so, for a full half-hour, after which he re-erupted into the sacristy. "Now what?" he asked me, arms akimbo. His face was red.

"Play it again?" I suggested brightly but pianissimo.

We were busily staring at each other in mutual frustration when in the distance we heard the sirens of police cars heading our way. Presently they wailed to a stop in front of the church, whereby we realized that Momma had coped. She had come to the wedding under full police escort, down Highway One at sixty, maybe seventy, miles an hour. Sam scuttled back to his organ bench and went into Wagner, or Mendelssohn, or whatever it is. Fortissimo.

Manifestly the traumas involved in that little incident were experienced by all, myself least of them, yet I still bear my scars and profit from my education. I can, in contrast, cite you an occasion when the burden fell upon me alone and remained unknown to all other participants. We can call it the Case of the Eight Parents.

Both the bride and the groom in this wedding must have been intrepid adventurers, for their respective parents were not only divorced but had also severally remarried. All eight of them came to the do. I cannot tell you how, or even if, they parcelled out the social functions surrounding a three-ring wedding—the rehearsal dinner, the wedding breakfast, etc. Under normal conditions the problem might have intrigued my interest, but at the moment I didn't care. I had a logistical puzzle of my own, an unprecedented problem of precedence.

How were those eight parents to be seated? How and in what pecking order was I to get these eight souls, and more especially their bodies, up the aisle and into what pews? Who outranked whom? Secreted in my study I shuffled them around, using chess men: bride's actual mother; that mother's present but unrelated and to my mind extraneous spouse; bride's actual father, estranged from bride's mother; bride's stepmother, unrelated but firmly affixed to the arm of the bride's father. Across the aisle on the groom's side the same situation prevailed.

Pastoral theology courses in seminary had not explored this problem in any depth. Etiquette books offered no help at all. Their up-to-date editions, more geared to modern society, may offer guidance, but as to that I neither know nor wish now to learn. The bishop was at a loss, too. I telephoned him, of course, to pick his considerable brains and vast experience, but he knew no more than I; he could only wish me well. I had to solve Rubik's Cube *de novo* and on my own. I did so, in my fashion, but you will not find the solution here. I forget what it is, or was. My only counsel, should you ever face a similar situation (heaven forfend a *double* wedding so compounded) is "Do something. Do it smoothly, yet firmly, hoping to create an illusion that you know what you're about."

Wedding trauma seems to be only somewhat proportional to the sheer physical size of the event but directly proportional to the number of participants and observers who come from out of town. Let's defer consideration of the latter and examine sheer size first.

I have been involved in some weddings so vast that front pews had to be removed from the nave to allow standing room for eighteen bridesmaids in hoopskirts and a balancing number of groomsmen, not so attired. This wedding climaxed such a round of secular celebrations as you might not believe, but if there were attendant blood-pressure problems, I never learned of them. The mother and father of the bride were able executives with cool heads, superior brains, excellent foresight, and sound basic training gained in the prior weddings of three other daughters. Most of the essential participants—good ushers are of the essence—were also veterans and, what is equally important, were locals. My only trepidation occurred as, during the Great Entrance, I stood there for an eternity watching those eighteen bridesmaids, each one lovelier than the last, enter at the west doors one after the other and proceed, with all deliberate speed and fixed smiles, up the aisle toward me.

I had rehearsed them. I knew exactly how many there were, yet they seemed an endless procession of beautiful clones, endlessly reproducing themselves before my startled eyes. My concern arose because at rehearsal they had not worn hoopskirts but simple party dresses. I had to wonder whether, here in real life, they would all fit into the space we had measured and created for them. They did, perfectly. In former years I had taught geometry, and my present calculations worked out well. Nothing in a clergyman's experience is irrelevant or wasted.

Weddings when half the party comes from out of town can be the real can of worms. Some of the attendant problems are minor and obvious enough. For the sake of completeness they will be outlined later, but we will start at the top:

The mothers of bride and groom have not met each other until eleven minutes before the rehearsal—one is from Boston, the other from Dallas, so how could they? Oh, there has been much cross-country telephoning and letter writing and comparisons of guest lists, including a character sketch of Aunt Isabel, before this blessed moment arrives, but only now do they meet live. On paper the bride's mother does outrank the groom's and is of course on somewhat local turf—she used to live here, indeed was married here; the present wedding is imported to continue that lovely tradition—but in the flesh a certain jockeying for position can occur, sometimes subtly, at times more overtly, right there before the altar. The polite struggle for priority, not to say personal identity, is of course compounded by the cultural disparities between Boston and Dallas.

The ladies having finally arrived at an understanding, the officiant now hears the dread news that the head usher's plane is late. From his point of view it might better have been hijacked. Now the head usher will miss the rehearsal, but he will indeed be at the wedding, in a strange situation and on strange ground. He is the wedding's indispensable man, its ringmaster, its traffic cop. He is out there where the action is, making it all go forward and mesh smoothly. If he forgets one least detail, like pushing that half-hidden button after having escorted the bride's mother to her pew, nothing further will happen. Sam can and possibly will keep on playing until some lesser usher sees the light, but the officiant is hopelessly remote, immured in the sacristy standing guard over the groom and best man. He is in the head usher's hands, and this presently absent one will have to be indoctrinated, all unwilling, tomorrow morning, if indeed he can be located and drafted at that time. All the rest of the entourage will then be at the country club, enjoying a swimming party which the head usher will be loathe to miss. The officiant's ulcer twinges as he thinks on these things.

His only alternative is, at rehearsal, to teach the lesser groomsmen the head usher's job, telling them to pass the word on while cavorting at the country club. They will say, "Oh, sure, we'll tell him. Chuck's pretty smart; catches on quick. Beside, I think he's been in a wedding once. No sweat, preacher. No sweat at all." The officiant has heard these words before. His ulcer acts up again.

Lesser trauma arise in these situations because too many people who actually manage to arrive in town at the proper time do not know where anything is or where it can be procured. Many of them did not realize that the locale was in a dry county. Some extras decide at the last minute to come along, creating reservation problems at the motels (on one such occasion we had nine overflow groomsmen sleeping in our basement, and the hours kept in connection with wedding festivities are fantastic). Most important among these lesser matters is the fact that the officiant does not know which of the strangers can be trusted. There is always a fun-loving Rover amongst them; which one is he? (You find that out later. He is the one who paints H-E-L-P on the soles of the groom's shoes, which are prominently displayed when he kneels for the final blessing. A local will not do this. He knows your standards, or at least that he must continue to live in the same town with you. The foreigner can slip away, back to Dallas, doubtless there to sin again.)

There are enough unavoidable external pressures surrounding a wedding; we do not need that added sort of thing. Along the nuptial road there are licenses, prenuptial counseling sessions, dressmakers, haberdashers, printers, engravers, florists, caterers, transportation, motel reservations, canceled reservations, parking problems, a ciphering organ, lunches, suppers, dinners, breakfasts, cocktail parties, toasts and speeches, golf foursomes, the guest list for each and every event, recording of gifts and their donors, telephoning, answering the telephone, meeting planes, worrying about the weather, and at every step coping with Murphy's Law. The process goes on for many weeks with the pressure building all the time. It can overwhelm the steadiest head, the bravest heart, the coolest nerves.

Sometimes it does. Late one Friday night as I was leaving my serene church, its darkness faintly illuminated by the glow of only the sanctuary lamp and a few flickering vigil lights, two young people entered. I knew them and they knew me, although they were not of my parish—around here everybody knows everybody else and considerable of his business. I certainly knew, from reading our newspaper, that the couple were to be married the next day in a neighboring suburban church, so in greeting them I wished the girl well and congratulated the young man.

"Thank you," he said. After a moment he went on. "We're just worn out, Father. It's been too much. Well, we love the atmosphere of your church, and we know it's never locked. So we slipped away after tonight's rehearsal dinner to be here by ourselves for a while. To be in this peace and quiet. Is that all right?"

I told them it was indeed all right and went away from there.

TWENTY-ONE

The Face Is Familiar

*I wouldn't have thought it possible for strangers
to reminisce, but it can be done.*

I remember having a pretty good memory, back in the days of Mr.
Addison Sims of Seattle—remember him? I remember memorizing
both *L'Allegro* and *Il Penseroso* in one fifty-minute high-school study
period, without any difficulty, just to while away the time. More to
the point, I remember remembering the passing stranger who had
sold our family a magazine subscription three months before. This
was a useful feat because, although it turned out that he hadn't
actually absconded with our money, he had certainly neglected to
turn it in to the company. I believe we were lying fallow in one of
his desk drawers; in any case we were not getting our magazine. One
night after dinner my mother mentioned this fact in a puzzled way,
and without looking up from my homework I said, "You ordered it
through a man named Walsh. He lives at 324 Academy Street. His
telephone number is 6814." Undoubtedly, my mother gave me the

glance of a parent who wonders what she has spawned, but she did try Walsh on the telephone and shortly afterwards we began getting our magazine. I do forget what it was. Perhaps *Collier's* or the *Literary Digest*.

I suppose my basic trouble now is that too much old furniture is stored away in memory's halls and too many people wander there in the cobwebby dark. Innocent victims of my personal population explosion, you might call them. When their faces are vaguely familiar I smile and tip my hat in passing, but often when I glance back as I prepare to cross the street, the lady is pointing me out to a policeman. That isn't too bad because I can just disappear into the traffic. It *was* bad, however, that time I eagerly followed a young woman into the lingerie department, full of the conviction that she had been a member of my congregation a dozen or so years ago. Unfortunately it wasn't the same girl at all. She was distantly polite about the whole thing, but I still cringe when I wonder what she's thinking now. I can only hope, without faith, that she isn't.

This kind of thing can easily be avoided. Granting that you do have to tip your hat on occasion, with practice you can do it abstractedly, remotely, without a leer. Better still, stop wearing hats. And you certainly don't have to follow young women into the lingerie department. Still, in spite of every diligence, I spend far too much time nowadays in warm conversation with people whose faces are familiar, and that's all. Since I'm very happy these days to let sleeping dogs lie, I can't believe that this shadowboxing is my fault. For example, I don't see how in the world I could have escaped those fifteen miserable minutes I spent on the corner yesterday morning talking heartily (I always talk extra heartily on these occasions) with an old acquaintance I couldn't place at all. As a matter of fact, I had seen him coming, I wanted no part of the rootless wraith, I immediately began admiring the work of a nonexistent skywriter, and I was buttonholed all the same. Well, you can't just run away— not with those big paws on your lapels, you can't—so we talked and kidded and laughed until, in the mercy of providence, a bus came along. It wasn't going my way, but I took it.

By the way, my friend turned out to be the amiable cop on the Lexington Avenue beat, down by the outdoor fruit market where we've been buying watermelons and peaches for years. ("Still doing business at the same old stand?" I had asked him in our forlorn game of hide and seek. He must think I'm quite a wit.) I'd have known him immediately—let me think so, anyway—if he'd only stayed put, instead of straying from my mental pigeon hole. Or even if he hadn't disguised himself, quite unfairly, in plain clothes. I finally figured him out at three-thirty in the afternoon, after which I was able to get down to my day's work, or the morning's crossword puzzle, I forget which.

The incident reminded me strongly of the time when the ghostly past tracked me into my own living room—more exactly, into my own study, where I had learned to sequester myself in the hope of keeping out of trouble. I was sitting there, minding my own business, reading the evening paper, when the doorbell rang. My son responded to it. He handled the visitors nicely enough, but because he was in a hurry to get back to his TV program, he didn't handle them thoroughly. He just brought the people in and stated, "Somebody to see you, Pop." He didn't ask their names.

Those are the last people who get into my house without giving their names, preferably in writing. I sat with them—a fine young man and a delightful girl—for something over an hour, and to this moment I don't know who they were. Oh, their faces were familiar. I even realized, finally, that they had loomed out of the mist of a decade ago, when we lived in another city. Nothing else, least of all their names, would come into focus. But they were so confident we were turning well-thumbed pages that I couldn't possibly dash the bloom off their cheeks. I sat and squirmed and fenced and prayed.

Fortunately there were interruptions. After twenty fuzzy minutes our telephone rang with a message for my wife—you may be sure that I leaped to answer it. I escaped to the kitchen, where I took in the solid homey scene going on at the sink, with my wife in soapsuds up to her elbows and my daughter slowly circling plates with a wet cloth and chattering about some hilarious happening

during assembly time at the high school. Their radar wasn't register-
ing my eyebrow signals, so I had to deliver the message and drift
back to the never-never land of my study.

Somewhat later my boy came through the looking glass, asking
for help with TV flopover. The respite proved to be merely a stay of
execution.

"Who are they?" I whispered to him.

"Who are who?" he piped.

"The people in there. And keep your voice down."

"Don't you know?" he asked. He looked at me very carefully.
"You've been talking with them half the night."

Back in the study I tried to cling to sanity by listening to the
solid sounds of the real world behind the gibbering of us ghosts—the
muted chatter in the kitchen, the nonmuted staccato of TV, the
steady ticking of the clock out in the hall. In spite of all my efforts
the gap between that land and this kept widening. The tide set
strong against me, the night fell, the fog rolled in, and I drifted out
on a featureless sea. Without a paddle.

Strangely, our conversation didn't seem to suffer. Adrift there in
our leaky boat, we appeared to be talking sense, to be asking
questions with actual meaning, to be reminiscing about realities. I
wouldn't have thought it possible for strangers to reminisce, but it
can be done. It takes its toll, but it can be done.

Eventually we parted, friends if still strangers. Out at their car
my callers shook my hand in hearty gratitude.

"You've always given us such a sense of security," the girl said.

"Yes, sir," the boy echoed. "You give us that good old solid
feeling."

When their car had driven away, I went back into the house and
locked the door behind me.

"Who was that?" my wife called.

I slumped into the nearest chair. "A couple on their honeymoon
trip," I said. "They just couldn't pass through here without stopping
in to see me."

"How nice. Who did you say they were?"

"I didn't say," I told her. "I don't know."

She came into the living room. "I'm afraid I didn't hear you," she said. "It sounded as if you said you didn't know."

I looked up at her out of glazed eyes. "I don't," I said. "I did, but I don't. I give them a sense of security, though. That's something. In fact, that's a great deal."

My wife cross-examined me for twenty minutes, but she didn't get anything out of me. There was, of course, nothing to get. I think she still believes I'm keeping something from her, and I only wish it were so.

I also wish I knew what to do about these involvements. It doesn't do any good to tell myself, firmly and definitely, that I've simply got to be straightforward and admit my blankness at the outset, before the mess gets hopeless. The truth is that I have a conciliatory, or craven, nature, and therefore my course through life cannot possibly be simple or straightforward. I recoil from squashing beetles, let alone people. I keep Christmas cards from "Emma and George," which would have a lot more meaning if they were signed "Adam and Eve." Under no conceivable circumstances could I ever say, "I'm sorry, friend, but I don't place you."

Once I tried disciplining my mind, but that doesn't work either. This was after I had introduced an old friend to a roomful of people as "Alexander Smith," for the good reason that I thought that was his name. After several introductions, he put me straight, I think a bit stiffly, because his name was actually "Smith Alexander." At the moment I managed the explanation that I have other close friends whose names are Alexander Jones and Mason Alexander (I really do, as it happens) and the similarities threw me off. With the situation thus tidied over, I began this thing of mental discipline.

Every time I was faced with another job of introducing that man—he was new in town, we moved in the same circles, and after all he had been a college classmate—I would rehearse the words "Smith Alexander" in my mind as preparation. Soon I would decide—I think anybody would—that the combination was imposs-ible and that "Alexander Smith" had to be correct. Then I would

191

remember that "Jones" and "Mason" came into the picture in some manner. Well, if you have ever fooled around with "Kelly and Sheets" for "Keats and Shelley," you know the mental confusion that develops. I would always end up with something weirdly wrong. Alexander Smith (if that's his name; I'm not entirely sure any more) has been avoiding me lately. This isn't difficult, you may be sure, because I'm careful, too, about staying on the opposite side of the room.

Against all this haunting of my mental house the only exorcism I have found of much value is an old dodge of my grandfather's. Grandfather was a clergyman who lived to a ripe old age and who in the course of the ripening had come in contact with a million people, more or less. Any one of this million, especially a female one, who met him twenty years after their last parting was quite capable of babbling joyfully that he was "dear old Doctor Edmunds, of course he was, and she would know him in a moment anywhere." Then she would want him to tell her who *she* was. Dante's *Inferno* should have a circle reserved exclusively for the likes of her. Maybe it does.

The old boy was at a hopeless disadvantage, of course, because there was only one of him—perfectly identifiable from his bald head, long beard, black clothes, round collar and all—while there was an amorphous million of her, identical as guppies. He was never at a loss, however. "You have a different hat on, my dear," he would say. "I wonder if you realize how much a woman's hat alters her appearance." He always got away with it, back in those days when women wore hats.

He used a variant of this gag the time he went to a church convention in Philadelphia, taking my wife along with him to share the gaiety. He was about eighty at the time, so he met people he hadn't seen for fifty years; he had to use the hat trick from morning to night. He also ran into another situation—people would mistake my then-twenty-eight-year-old wife for his own younger daughter, my mother. "And this must be little *Margaret!*" they would cry, with rising inflection.

For a while grandfather got a lot of pleasure out of saying, slowly and deliberately so that every word would carry across the decades, "No, this is little Margaret's . . . second son's . . . wife." However, it didn't satisfy him to keep this up forever, or even for very long. On the third day of the convention, possibly when he began to tire of many things and many people, grandfather changed his pitch to, "No, this isn't little Margaret. This is little *Mary*." That's my wife's name, all right, but it is also the name of my grandfather's other, older, daughter—my Aunt Mary, who has some thirty-five years and eighty pounds on my wife. Grandfather just let his old friends take it from there. He said that a lot of them slipped away to take long looks at themselves in mirrors. Naturally the ravages of the years stared sadly back at them while over there at grandfather's right hand little Mary bloomed afresh.

This rocking people back on their heels at such times is a sound ploy, which I am definitely going to utilize. However, it leaves at least one loose end dangling. A moment ago when I answered the telephone a hearty voice came booming over the wire. "Hello there!" it cried. "This is John!" We had a very good connection, electrically speaking, but I must know fifty Johns and several Jons.

You would cope with that by simply saying "John who?" or "What John?" I wish I shared your forthright character and clearcut ways, but I don't. As it always does when I open my mouth, my foot flew automatically into it. "Hey there, John!" I cried happily. "How are you? Delighted to hear from you. Tell me all about everything!"

John proceeded to do so, at considerable length. I now know a great deal about him, but one prime fact still eludes. I don't know who he is.

TWENTY-TWO

Funerals

. . . funerals are held at 11 A.M., *2* P.M., *and 4* P.M.
so that undertakers may undertake three in one day.

The overnight railroad journey from Asheville to New York City used to be a thing of beauty and a joy—you could look up the details in Thomas Wolfe's *Of Time and the River*. On many occasions we reveled in it. In late-middle afternoon we entrained at Biltmore Station just as Tom Wolfe used to do (it's now a restaurant) and settled in to enjoy the trip down the mountains, through the tunnels, past the geysers, and onto the piedmont. Around Hickory we began to think about dinner, so we could savor it unhurriedly as the shadows lengthened in the still remaining daylight. We dined amid crispy napery and sparkling crystal as time and distance flowed benignly by.

The porter had made up our beds while we were thus luxuriating. We retired early, dozed and half-wakened off and on throughout a clickety-clackety swaying night, and rose equally early the next morning, giants refreshed with wine, at Grand Central—or was it Penn Station?

Things were otherwise when I had to take the trip in order to attend my grandfather's funeral, in the midst of World War II. Thirteen of us, with our baggage, made the first half of the journey standing on the open platforms between two cars. During the second half there were only twelve of us. In the middle of the night and of Virginia, where the train stopped to back and fill and linger for the umpteenth inexplicable time, a drunken and befuddled soldier in our party wanted off. Without discussion we assisted his desire and made sure to hand his duffel bag down to him. I must leave him and it standing there in the dark. I have not the remotest idea what happened to him after that, but I do know that the remaining dozen of us appreciated the freedom of extra room that his sudden whim made available to us on our platforms.

Grandfather's funeral was held in Newark, New Jersey, in the great downtown church where he had, back at the turn of the century, been rector; where my mother had grown up; where my father became organist and so had met her; where they were married; where in good time I also was; and where I was ordained. The tears came to my eyes as, riding in my family's car toward it, we rounded the corner on Broad Street and the solid foursquare building came in sight, radiating the strength and purpose of eternity.

Inside, after a look around, I had to brush my eyes again. For twenty-five years, after he had left that parish, my grandfather had been Professor of New Testament at the General Theological Seminary in New York—"my" seminary in due time. Its dean was there officiating. Its faculty were there, assisting and attending. I forget how many bishops were or how many other clergy, come from all parts of the country in affection, respect, and thanksgiving for one man's life and work. I also was able to recognize many of the laity, distinguished citizens of the city and of the state, who had gathered together there for the same reason. In that company, from that company, the old familiar, ever new, time-steeped liturgical words thundered like a mighty flood.

Much the same experience was granted me some decades later, when back in Asheville we laid to rest the bishop of the diocese at the end of his long service there. As it happened he and I had been on a fishing trip—both for souls and for the finny variety—the weekend before. As we tossed our lures, we discussed other such trips during his approaching retirement, which would begin some six months later. We parted on a Monday, he to return straight home to his beloved work and I, already in retirement, to do so by a more circuitous route. The telephone may have been ringing when, later on Wednesday, I came into my house. If it wasn't, it soon did. The bishop had just died. His funeral was a tribute equal to that other one of so many years before and for like reasons.

I must suppose there still are giants in the earth, still doing their gigantic deeds. There had better be. We have lost a great many recently, and the world cries out for their kind.

This seems the place to state an apparent contrast. It will tell of a funeral—Catherine's—attended not by hundreds but only (to the naked eye) by my wife and myself, the officiant. For years my wife had tended that simple, that strange and wonderful lady whose Pennsylvania family had found bothersome and had shipped off to Florida to be out of sight, out of mind, out of money, and ultimately to die. My wife discovered Catherine—she came to church twice on Sundays—and took her under her wing. I spare you the details of the passing years as they slowly closed in around that unusual, that lonely, that forgotten and pauperized soul. I will merely say that once I wrote her sibling, her next of kin, in Philadelphia, that city of brotherly love, asking him to come down and take charge, but if he couldn't or wouldn't, to (1) send a power of attorney and (2) send money. I remember the exact words of his note in reply (wrapped around a crumpled dollar bill): "Keep up the good work, brother." I will add that Catherine's face was, physically speaking, plain to the point of near-ugliness. That is to say, it was while she lived. When she learned she was dying, her joy in the news transfigured her. She became beautiful.

197

With that too-skimpy background I take you to the funeral that crowned her days. The funeral director, a friend of ours, contributed his professional attention, a suitable dress, a casket, and a final resting place after my wife had told him the whole story. My wife set her own favorite earrings on the wizened body of that greatly loved and faithfully tended soul. The two of us then laid all to rest and had you been watching, you would have thought that only two had known and cared and come, at the end of a long and gracious human life, to note the turning of a page in an eternal story.

I am persuaded that you would have been wrong. I believe there was a host of witnesses, that angels and archangels and the whole company of heaven were there. I feel that they wouldn't have missed that opportunity for the world and that they took Catherine with them when they left, after all was finished here below. The rest of us might meet her again sometime, if we're good.

Surely it is only proper, even unavoidable, to have a thing about funerals when you have a thing about human life. As John Donne pointed out long ago, people enrich us while they are here beside us, and their departing is a personal impoverishment, a loss of a part of oneself. In that measure the funeral bell tolls for thee. Additionally, reverence for the mystery of life demands reverence for the mystery of death and gets it. Down our way cars automatically pull over to the shoulder of the road and stop until the funeral procession en route to the cemetery has passed by. Pedestrians also stop. Hats are removed. I imagine it's the same where you live. Everyone stands still, in awe and in tribute and in prayer.

Thus, when in the course of ministering in any largish city we clergy are called upon by a funeral director who asks if we will bury a nameless waif with no identifiable ecclesiastical connections, we assure him that of course we will, generally adding the jocular ritual phrase, "I'd be glad to bury a Baptist every day." (The Baptist preacher doubtless expresses the same witticism, substituting the word "Episcopalian.") In sober truth we have no interest whatsoever in private brands. Even if we had started out, some years before, with exclusive notions about devoting our lives in ministry to the chosen people, we soon learned that all people are chosen. Once, indeed, after I had interred a probable Mohammedan, assisted by an obviously genuine Jewish undertaker, I told the latter to feel free to call on me any time he had difficulty locating an available parson. My meaning was that I would not want any body laid to eternal rest without proper rites. I believe he thought I was a ghoul, interested in the ten-dollar honorarium. Certainly I never heard from him again. In short, we are all one with my priest friend, rector of a fashionable parish, who when taken to task by his senior warden for having buried a Negro and asked why he did so, replied, "Because he was dead."

By the way, all or nearly all the funeral directors I have had dealings with have been a fine lot, compassionate and cooperative as well as efficient and able. After all, they do depend on good will and repeat business, but that is a horrid way to put it. The truth is that they genuinely wish to serve their communities and on that firm base build honored institutions which endure from generation to generation. I have even had them call me in to dress the body of a priest in eucharistic vestments when they did not know how that was done. The casket was never going to be opened, of course, but they wanted to get things right. On one such occasion I had to contribute those vestments from my own scanty supply. Once again the casket would never be opened, but one really does want to get things right.

For that same reason I have never, over the course of nearly half a century and probably a thousand burials, permitted it to rain on the mourners and me during any interment. Once I did have a close call. The clouds were lowering, but rain held off until I concluded and stepped aside. It poured down when the Methodist minister took over in our joint effort, but that was in his jurisdiction.

Speaking of Methodists reminds me that I once borrowed their large church in order to bury a Kansas pioneer, a leading light in our community from before the bad old days of the county seat fights. According to legend he had a couple of notches on his handgun. He was my parishioner, but I strongly suspected that our tiny building would not accommodate those who would come to see him off. Sure enough, at the hour of his funeral the whole town shut down. All five hundred of its citizens were there as I held forth with the grand old words. My wife told me later that one of the Methodist ladies in the pew ahead of her leaned to a companion and hissed, "Those Episcopalians stole our Prayer Book." The observation lacked historical foundation, as you know. In actual fact, they stole ours.

I have often ruminated on what they had not time to teach us in seminary. I never learned that I would have the privilege of helping dig a grave in stubborn soil and, later, in full wind-blown vestments, of helping carry a casket up the steep rocky hill leading to that cemetery. I never learned there that a requiem mass follows—does not precede—the burial office; I learned that later, the hard way. They did not teach us the proper techniques for scattering ashes after a cremation—off the end of a borrowed dock; in waders, on a tidal flat; from an airplane flying over the Atlantic Ocean; in a mountain stream after crawling through chigger-infested under-brush. They omitted to disclose that funerals are held at 11 A.M., 2 P.M., and 4 P.M. so that undertakers may undertake three in one day and so that on occasion we clergy can too. They gave no counsel about multiple funerals—say of half a family simultaneously wiped out in a boating accident. They offered no comment on pastoral care during the months of waiting, in high altitudes during a bitter winter, for the earth to thaw sufficiently so that, using dynamite and a backhoe, a grave might be dug and a finality be accomplished.

Of course they did not teach those and other things. Who can foresee all, or even a few, of the permutations and combinations of that multifaceted and ever-fascinating adventure, human life and death. One has to live and learn, then to die and continue learning.

TWENTY-THREE

Facing Forty

. . . she died but was not buried at age forty.

In these rapidly written words I shall probably sound as strident as a common scold, and thus be hoist by my own petard. If so my reason, or excuse, is that I have just returned from an hour spent with a lady whom I shall call Mrs. Grimes, and I am sick at heart. Sick not only because of her, but also because she represents an increasingly large section of the human race. If she is what a human being becomes as the years go by, how futile life is. Eons of evolution, millenia of life, centuries of civilization—and all there is to show is Mrs. Grimes.

You know her kind. She is a fading widow, about seventy years old. A couple of decades ago she was happy and adjusted, but now nothing in her existence is right. The weather is bad, the food is poor, the service is slovenly, the minister does not call, no doctor understands her case, the TV is vulgar, modern literature is decadent, people are standoffish, and the clocks do not keep good time.

This plaintive monologue, which she considers to be a conversation, pours forth in one continual whine, neatly exposing her inner life.

The Mmes. Grimes are on the increase; modern medical improvements make it difficult for their bodies to die. We are doomed to see a lot more of her kind because of the increasing span of human life. So, beyond inducing nausea, she frightens me. Not in herself, the poor old walking corpse, but for what she symbolizes. She is what is going to happen to some of my friends as they grow older, unless they're careful. She might happen to you. She might happen to me.

But she needn't happen to you or me if, warned by her plight, we learn the philosophy of the second half of life. Mrs. Grimes demonstrates that human life is divided into two distinct parts, with a far-reaching change of life occurring around forty. This change is vastly more than physical; it is so basic that each half of life has its own distinct governing philosophy.

The manner of life during the first forty years is fairly simple for us to follow, as it is directed by nature. One's energy is called upon by physical necessity—the need to work, raise money, support a family, secure a sound footing in his or her chosen society. Most of us do these things according to our particular abilities and opportunities—even Mrs. Grimes negotiated her first forty years successfully. We see Nature's plan clearly, or at least we instinctively respond to it because of its sheer compulsion. So we buckle down and, in our measure, we attain our goals. We find a vocation or it finds us, we achieve a certain amount of ease in it, we may even rise in it. We establish a home, furnish it, raise and educate our children, make friends, have our neighbors in for dinner. From time to time, we may realize that these solid and satisfying gains are acquired at the cost of certain aspects of our personality, that society rewards what we do rather than what we are. But the fleeting thought does not trouble us greatly. We shrug away the bothersome idea—and we do so without incurring psychic danger—with the unfortunately true observation that living in this material world necessitates compromise.

Then comes the second half of life, sooner than we expected. At that point, Mrs. Grimes just continued shrugging, saying "So what?" In so doing, she made the mistake of her life. She did not realize that the entire philosophy of the second span must be different from that of the first; happiness during the latter half of life cannot come the same way it did during the first half. Doubtless she had heard that life begins at forty. But she didn't interpret this as meaning that a whole new *kind* of life then begins, and that it must be attacked from an entirely different angle. Culture, instead of necessity, governs the second half of life.

Achievement, solidity, social usefulness, adequate material security—all the valid goals of youth—can be pursued as the dominating aim of life after forty only at the cost of constant diminution of personality. Of course, they must still be pursued, or one would starve; but the fierceness of the chase must slacken and the first place must be yielded to something else. This is true primarily because the individual is dealing with a new person, a changed person with different needs to be satisfied lest he or she be stultified. A human being, by definition, is not simply a rather interesting animal—a human being also has a spirit. Around the middle of life that spirit stirs, wakens from its long sleep. From then on, personality, rather than achievement, must be the prime pursuit. It is as if Mrs. Grimes's subconscious mind called to her on the morning of her fortieth birthday: "What about *me*, now? You've been spending your energy on the *things* of life—but what shall it profit a woman to gain the whole world and lose her soul?" Mrs. Grimes, unfortunately, paid no heed and so became involved in futility.

Proof of this far-reaching change of life is found in statistical charts. When do the peaks occur in the graphs of mental breakdown? In two places: as adolescence passes into youth, shortly after puberty; and as youth fades into middle age, in the later thirties. The too-frequent neurotic disturbances of the latter bracket reveal the consistent human effort to carry the youthful point of view beyond its time. The grown man who escaped the first danger and passed safely from adolescence to adult life is now shrinking from the demands of life's afternoon.

That is what statistics show. Individual illustrations are legion. Mrs. Grimes is one I know; another I will call Mr. Osgood. The poor fellow is so absorbed by his work that he is no more human than one of the machines in his own plant. When he has nothing else to do—which is always because he is afraid to be alone with his dying personality—he's at the shop, working.

He claims he has to work all the time because living is expensive. Far be it from me to deny that fact, but the real point is that life itself is very dear. Mr. Osgood's solvency or insolvency doesn't alter the facts of his evolving nature. Even if he has not achieved security at forty, he must turn his main attention in another direction. We might inquire of Mr. Osgood when he expects to begin living, as opposed to making a living, but I'm afraid we would be met only by further rationalization. Mr. Osgood, like anyone who, at his age, refuses to relegate the admitted problem of physical security to its then proper place, is vainly trying to keep his new wine in old bottles. And the wine is turning sour; it is becoming whine. Imagine what his wife thinks of the situation and what she probably will do about it. Mr. Osgood is only fifty, but his wife believes it's already too late for him to start becoming a human being.

Another case in point we will call Mr. Barnes. I met Jim Barnes again at our twenty-fifth college reunion. I had liked the fellow as an undergraduate; he was one of the leading spirits in our class. Now he is simply a bore. During the reunion, he continually harked back to the exploits of our student days until his circle of weary hearers drifted away, leaving him to his solitary and pathetic cheerleading. Mr. Barnes is now a bore, as stated. Soon he will be worse than that—a hermit. And the ultimate pity is that he, like Mrs. Grimes and Mr. Osgood, will never know what happened to him. He may have a vague suspicion that the laws of life he once trusted have now failed. But I suspect he will feel that life itself has failed.

Life does not fail; life demands. Individuals fail. They do so when they shrink from the demands of the new era. Adults fail when they refuse to face the demand of the second half of life.

What demand? The demand of paying attention to oneself. Just as young people must self-forgetfully spend themselves, achieve practical results, and acquire happiness as a byproduct of external activity, so aging people, to avoid frustration, are under nature's compulsion to give serious attention to themselves.

In a word, when we are reasonably at ease in the developed pattern of our physical security, we must devote our main energies to culture. I call it that—but it can as easily be called the study of man, or what you will. It means involvement in arts and hobbies, in religion and the mysteries of life, in thought and literature, in all forms of creation—spiritual rather than physical, in the cultivation of personality.

Painting would have saved Mrs. Grimes. Refinishing antique furniture would have helped her, too. Zealous and interested gardening might have been a way out—or a way *in*. So might writing poetry. Or studying one of the sciences. She could have bought a book on astronomy and lifted her thoughts to the stars. But it is pointless to enumerate the particular aspects of culture she might have followed, for anything that led her into the unlimited world of the spirit's aspirations would have saved her from her present misery. Had she thrown the main energies of her life into any of these things, she would have responded to what the second half of life demands. She would have been an ever-growing woman, increasingly joyful and stimulating. Her soul would have been at peace with itself because she was conforming to the laws of human destiny. Instead, she died but was not buried at the age of forty.

Those who are approaching forty must realize that this new kind of life is dawning. The afternoon of life is not simply an ever-weakening adjunct to life's vigorous morning; it is not merely a time to carry forward, with our diminishing strength, the activities of our younger days. Rather, it is a time to center on those things our awakening spirit urges us. A time to rake the ashes from the banked fire of personality so that it may burst into flame. The only remaining difficulty will be to find time for an investigation of all the intriguing possibilities.

TWENTY-FOUR

Creativity

"There is a god in us;
he stirs and we grow warm."—Ovid

In the normal course of pleasureable duty my wife and I had been entertaining some youngsters at supper one Sunday and were just sitting around after the meal, jabbering in a familiar group, when out of the blue and in one instantaneous flash a complete six-thousand-word short story formed itself in my mind and insisted upon being born full-grown. The pent-up pressure would not be denied nor long contained. As soon as I decently could, I sent those young people about their business, rushed to my typewriter, and set it to smoking. For the next few hours I wasn't engaged in automatic writing, as I understand that term, yet in one continuous session without any hesitations or groping for words I gave that story its release on paper. It went into final manuscript form the next morning without any changes, received immediate acceptance (over the transom, yet!) by the old *Saturday Evening*

Post, and has been doing nicely ever since.

I did, and still do, find that a startling creative experience that I could hope might happen again, yet I do not set store by it. Partly I don't because experience assures me flatly that most of the time—99.44 percent of the time in the early stages of our development—creative results follow hard and painfully upon the application of the seat of the pants to the seat of the chair. (In my case they flow best when I am lying flat on my back on a couch, in the free-association psychiatric position. I have often wished for a typewriter that could be suspended upside down from the ceiling above me there so that I could write in my free-floating position with a minimum of mechanical interference between the mind and the matter. Getting up and going to the desk somehow inhibits me a bit, leaves something behind, so that which comes out at the desk isn't as good as the stuff of the couch.) The other reason I am not completely led astray by that experience is that genuine creativity requires our cooperation. Make that "graciously permits" our cooperation. That's at the very heart of its nature.

I hasten to say that I'm quite certain we never will, never can, fully understand the intriguing mystery of creativity—of inspiration's flash and perspiration's productivity. However, there is no law inhibiting wonderments about the subject, which in my case began years ago when as a young boy I watched my father composing music. Naturally I knew he was a pianist and organist of the highest ability, who had developed his inborn musical talent (whence come such things?) by years of study and discipline. I had also heard about his achievements and recognition in the musical world before early deafness put an end to his career as a performer. In youth's simplistic fashion I took it as only natural that he had then turned to composing. Yet even youth had to wonder how it was possible for a deaf man to hear or to dream up mental melody. Where did the music come from, anyway? Was it inside his head all the time or, as with a radio, did he have to tune in to something outside? If so, how did he do that, and how did the music get from outside in, particularly since he had a sound barrier? Furthermore, when he wrote it

208

down as queer marks on oddly lined paper, how did he know it was the theme and the harmony he was imagining? And then if somebody turned the queer marks back into sound, would it be the same thing that my father had either overheard or dreamed up?

Those are good questions, but here toward the end of life's span I tend to ignore them in favor of marveling that human creativity exists; that we can make positive contributions in the field of the good, the beautiful, and the true. I rejoice that genuine creativity comes from God and goes to God—that it always affirms and builds. What more could we really want?

Some of our creative Great Ones—vastly gifted immortals hugely responsive to their talents—apparently overhear the very music of the spheres and bring it down to earth for our eternal enrichment. The rest of us seem limited to assembling a few of the things we find lying around right here. As the fellow said, what then results is our contraption, not our creation. Yet Thomas Higginson has pointed out that "Originality is a pair of fresh eyes." And history reports an unending supply of fresh eyes which, having seen things from a different angle, enable their owners to evolve new works of art and inventions from their stimulated thoughts and inspiration. I call this lesser process and these lesser products creativity, too, although I realize that in so doing I open the door to rhapsodies about "the latest Paris creations" and "Mr. Anthony's creative coiffures."

Mr. Anthony has something to be said for him, anyway. Surely we cannot validly limit "originality," "inventiveness," and the like to productions emanating from the "higher" media: horsehair and catgut, or taut wires and felt hammers, or pigmented egg yolk and canvas. Surely creativity can employ a penknife and a block of basswood, or a collection of coat hangers and old tin cans, or broomstraw and ribbons, or any of the thousand and one other media we see at the Craftsman's Fair and many others that we don't, just as properly as it can find outlet through a potter's wheel, with a word processor, or on the dramatic boards. In truth there may well be no definable limits to the myriad modes of healthy self-expression—including human hair as well as camel's. A prejudice of mine may compel Mr. Anthony to submit his own brief on this matter, but I would be happy to extol the originality of my neighbor with his inventive saber saw and electric drill. Certainly you can come to my house and appreciate the self-expressive uses of interior decorating, followed by a savoring of the creative potential in spices and herbs. As a matter of fact, I believe I have watched artistic talent expressing itself astride a bulldozer on a construction job. I have to conclude that the medium doesn't essentially matter. One must master it, so that it is a fluid extension of oneself, and some expressive outlets are indeed far more subtle, demanding, and rewarding than others, but, surely in the last analysis, to each his own.

Our broad use of words, which isn't confining "creativity" to the rare genius and its medium to a symphony orchestra, involves the ready-made kindred assertion that all of us humans are potentially creative and most of us are actually so. Michelangelo's Adam, to whose hand from God's finger a spark is about to jump, is Everyman, a chip off the old block. Ovid states the same truth in his lovely words, "There is a god in us; he stirs and we grow warm." It fascinates and cheers me that pure energy—the life force—God—surges irresistibly into everyone of us and must find its release.

Admittedly this is also true of robins in nest-building time and of blackberry bushes in July, but no one expects a robin to build a Parthenon in his backyard nor berry bushes to yield crêpe suzettes. It's otherwise with people, who continually surprise us by doing the darnedest things at the darnedest times. Not simply on a rare day in June does the veriest human clod feel a stir of might, an instinct within him that reaches and towers. He is continually being given far more life than he needs for mere living, and it insists upon bursting out somewhere, somehow, the while carrying him himself along with it. Doubtless as the shadows lengthen and the evening comes, and the busy world is hushed and the fever of life is over, our creative work here is done and we know peace at last. Yet only death can finally quench the fitful flickering fire. While the self lives, it must express itself by at least building a sand castle on the seashore because the trumpet keeps on sounding from the hid battlements of eternity, and hearing it however faintly, we must respond however clumsily. So it is no new thing that everywhere today there is a vast yearning among people for the opportunity to feel significant as individuals—to be themselves, to express themselves, to do their own things. This is simply the name of the human game because it is the name of the divine game, as we shall shortly suggest.

Before doing so we must pause to rejoice that we are not automata, that the life force doesn't do the whole creative job. As was hinted at the outset, the hardest kind of cooperative work is required of our free will, especially in our beginning years. Indeed, often a flow of inspiration then seems not merely to follow upon but actually to result from a copious flow of perspiration. And at no stage of our development can matter exist without form. One simply must build a solid rock foundation in order to support his castle in the air, and usually that's done stone by heavy stone, by dint of much chipping and shaping, occasionally accompanied by grief and groaning as one labors to get things just right.

Happily, as a person is thus brooding and agonizing over his work, an alternating current can come into being. Feedback begins between the emerging creation and its creator, much as it does between adjacent logs in a smoldering fire, each borrowing flame from the other until they burst into unexpected blaze. That is to say, the creative process is itself potentially creative and can raise a project to utterly unforeseen levels. Don Quixote is a classic example of this alchemy. As the story moves forward, Cervantes is progressively transmuted, and his every character glows more and more golden on each new page.

We'll return to this point heavy-handedly and at length, on increasingly higher levels, but before we do let me insert another personal reminiscence for its illustrative values. During our family's two-week vacation at Bill's ranch, I had set myself the chore of producing at least one salable story or article (one of my children was in the clutches of the orthodontist at the time, and the other was frequenting the dermatologist, so financial necessity was hard upon us—financial necessity does seem to play a part in this business). I did have some ideas stored up, and for several days at the ranch applied myself diligently to their expression. None of them would jell. Despite persevering drudgery, every start turned out to be a false one that petered out into nothing. Ultimately, one morning after a couple of frustrating hours I ripped a hopeless sheet of paper out of the typewriter, inserted a fresh one from sheer habit, and sat back wearily with my brain out of gear. My eyes began idly following the ranch guests cavorting in the riding ring below me. Soon my mind joined this observation because something in the antics and the conversation of the riding group had caught its fancy. Shortly my fingers started to rove the typewriter's keys on an unpremeditated tack. Characters, events, and a story line began to take form on the paper, rather to my astonishment. Increasingly interested in this developing world, I abandoned the ring-riders and devoted my whole attention to watching my newborn brain-children and recording their doings. By lunch time I was able to tell my wife that I seemed to be at last on my way although I didn't know yet where I was going. Perhaps I'd have something solid to report at dinner; meanwhile I wouldn't be joining the trail ride scheduled for that afternoon. I'd keep on writing.

By cocktail time that story was finished. *Good Housekeeping* accepted it at once and asked for another one like it, using the same characters. This invitation ultimately led to a whole book filled with those people, but that's another story—in fact a lot of other stories, involving hard work over a number of years. More to the present point is that after an inner current stirred and began to flow that morning at the ranch, it continued to rise and swell until it broke my logjam completely. I was able to start another article that same evening, to finish it the next morning, and to begin still a third sketch that next afternoon. Perspiration had apparently greased the launching skids, fatigue had perhaps also served to get me out of my own way, and that mysterious alchemy began its process.

It seems germane to note additionally that those days of blockage and facility at the ranch were spent sitting under a pine tree alone, removed from family, friends, and fun. Creativity surely involves return and withdrawal. One must immerse himself deeply in the stream of life, then go sit by himself, dripping wet, at the side of the river for a time. We can't create without there having been involvement, nor yet while we are wholly involved, spending all our energies in other directions—for example, I have never found it possible to write during the first couple of years in a new job, while applying myself single-mindedly to getting it in hand. Gestation requires fertilization and then time, leading toward a lonely confinement when one labors solely in that particular creativity.

High-level creativity seems supremely to be a function of the solitary self; a committee can collaborate in producing only the ungainly camel. It seems necessary in view of the facts, however, to treat this dogmatism gingerly and with certain qualifications. Clearly there is such a stimulating thing as creative tension; blazing sparks do fly from the flint and steel of heated minds opposed. Furthermore, two or more people—a man and wife, say, or a family— and only two or more people can create an atmosphere mutually stimulating to individual creativity. In addition, it is true that books have been written by two authors, each producing half of the chapters like Thurber and White in writing "*Is Sex Necessary?*" Immortal pairs like Gilbert and Sullivan have successfully linked two different media in a single whole. And that perhaps most significant creating in the world—a new human life—is only possible through the lusty cooperation of two partners. Yet when all is said about the seminal clash of views, about the fruits of discussion, about the fertility of brainstorming groups, about the whole being greater than the sum of its parts, the fact does seem to remain that ultimately some lonely individual has to retire into his closet, shut the door, and labor in solitary confinement. It does take two to tango, but other creativity worthy of the name seems to be a process entrusted to an individual self. Even the eternal and undivided Trinity, we are told by St. John, brought the Creation to pass through the sole agency of One Person.

That having been done in the large, the ever-ongoing activity of the Creator then flows through us in the small, whereby it is seen that the really true and ultimate purpose of our creative activity, like God's, is to be creative of *us*.

In a previous chapter we noted that a master bowyer, discerning the bow latent within a billet of yew, carefully cuts away all excess and liberates the captive at the heart. Similarly, God's drawknife and sandpaper (hey, that hurts!) separate us from the elements that imprison us. But a human being is not like the bowyer's wood clamped supinely there to be worked upon from the outside alone. Made in the image and likeness of God, which essentially means endowed with creative abilities too, we cooperate from within, as it were, with His loving labors upon us.

Here, I think, is the final glory in the whole lovely mystery of creativity. On this level, sawdust *is* incense. That is to say, a created object is recognized as being a love letter sent to God; and our creative desires are seen to be God-given yearnings Godward. "There is a god in us. . . ." It is realized that our striving for the infinite, which is the essence of creativity, carries us beyond ourselves toward the waiting God.

TWENTY-FIVE

Fringe Benefits

. . . exactly the right person at precisely the right time.

This is a day during which there arrived at our retirement digs, out of the blue, two letters from parishioners of long ago and far away. For full forty years I had not heard from one of the writers; it had been twenty-five years in the case of the other. Both began by recalling mutual experiences in the past and then brought me up to date about the present. Yesterday, too, a former parishioner broke a silence of two decades by telephoning while in a neighboring city to thank me for alleged good deeds done once upon a time and then to chat a while about this, that, and the other. Thus I am reminded, among other things, that today is the last day of spring, a cool one up here in the mountains. Soon our summer visitors—those that have not already arrived; we're having dinner with one couple tomorrow—from Florida and other Southern hotspots will be making their annual pilgrimage here, and we will be renewing many other old acquaintances as they stop by or stay over. We eagerly await the influx, the renewal, the picking up exactly where we left off with old friends and coworkers. Perhaps among them will be that couple with whom my wife and I sat up in our car all night outside a hospital window watching the shadow of the neurosurgeon moving across the frosted window of the operating room as he worked slowly and delicately inside their daughter's brain after an automobile accident. Around 3:00 A.M. her father, my high-church senior warden, had lapsed into the language of his Georgia Baptist boyhood, saying "Let's have another word of prayer." It, or the surgical team, or both together, were completely efficacious. That beautiful daughter now has three lovelies of her own.

A few weeks ago my wife and I attended Alumni Day at the boarding school where I had been chaplain in the 1940s. One of the boys from that era is the present headmaster; another has been a faculty member there for a quarter of a century and more. Several of the returning Old Boys from that same period are now on the school's Board of Directors; one is its Chairman. Proudly he showed us around the whole familiar thousand-acre campus, calling our special attention to the new gymnasium and athletic complex, the improved administration building, the refurbished dormitories, the expanded science laboratories, the new faculty houses. The whole place looked great. He then told us of the Endowment Fund's overflowing success and in eager words outlined plans for the future.

They too look great, as do the Old Boys. They are in their fifties now, but seem eternally young and certainly are supremely active. One of them is a shipping tycoon down New Orleans way. Another is deep in Texas oil. Two are presidents of internationally known textile firms in the Carolinas, and several others are among this country's leading industrialists. One is creatively at work out in Hollywood. Still another, until his recent and most untimely death, was dean at one of our Church's seminaries.

When I was headmaster at that school in the seventies, I had experienced the sorrowful necessity of expelling the son of one of my Old Boys only a few months prior to his graduation. He was and is a

216

superior young man who had, to everyone's deep distress, run up against one of the school's inflexible regulations close to the end of his senior year. His very seniority lay at the heart of the matter. Seniors, in or out of school, are not simply "expected to know better," as the dreadful expression has it. They are privileged to exercise authority, and privilege begets responsibility. At all times they are to embody, hence to exemplify and command, the highest and the best.

My Old Boy knew—knows—this in his very bones. Upon arriving in great grief to gather in his son, he had nothing but sincere respect for the school's time-honored standards, commendation for our having done the only proper thing, and continuing love for his son. He remains one of the school's strongest supporters and greatest benefactors. He and the others are making—have made— it one of the nation's truly great formative institutions.

We visited with all the other mature alumni there—college professors, clergymen, executives, farmers, businessmen, bankers, lawyers—who called me "Pop" as in the old days of my chaplaincy, and with the younger ones from my more recent stint as headmaster, who called me "Sir." They all are men of high standards and solid integrity in a world that needs their kind of leadership and, through them, is getting it. Because of them, the great institution which helped to mold them sheds its light all over the country.

Before leaving at the end of the day, my wife and I visited the school's chapel. This oldest and only remaining original building on the campus stands, literally and symbolically, in the center of the whole, where it always has been and where it will always remain. Stained-glass windows in it are dedicated to the memory of the founders, of former headmasters, and of students killed in various of our nation's wars. The ashes of several of them are in a columbarium in the attached smaller chapel.

So are those of one of the greatest men I have ever known, the school's athletic director for more than fifty years. Throughout half a century he coached every sport the school engaged in. He liked to win, and his teams did win, but he did not think that winning was everything, much less that it was the only thing. He thought that the *way* you won was everything. You gave your adversary every consideration, every courtesy, even every advantage, and then when you licked him you could properly enjoy a proper satisfaction. In short he didn't teach football, or basketball, or baseball, or track. He taught boys. When he was through with them, they were men. I know his ashes are in that chapel because I put them there, but I would be thus aware in any case because their stalwart presence remains a palpable thing. In that chapel my wife and I especially remembered the travails of our souls there at that school, and we were satisfied.

Let me say it again in so many words: *people* are the greatest fringe benefit as we go our individual ways through life. While the sun shines, the familiar others on pilgrimage by our sides are our daily bread. At night they are guiding stars in our dark sky. Along with them, because of them, we can go our journey with steady purpose, with bravery, and often with great joy. "It is not good . . . that man should be alone," and so in the providing of God we are not. A supreme joy of long life spent in one general locale is that we have solid friendships going back thirty, forty, fifty years and more. Some still live just down the street and have wandered through these pages. Others, for example, astrophysicist Johnston Cocke, codiscoverer of the pulsar optically, and author Gail Godwin, grew up in my Asheville parish but have long since moved on to other spheres. So their two ships drew alongside mine from astern, followed a close parallel course for a while, then put on full sail and took off for uncharted seas. From time to time, however, they send back tidings about what's going on 'way out yonder. Better still, occasionally they visit home again, and we can talk things over. Several of Godwin's acute suggestions have thus found expression in a couple of my books (including this one) which she graciously read in early manuscript. Thus it goes with all of us.

From time to time God also provides a bonus in the shape of a new planet or comet that swims, however briefly, into our ken.

Through exposure to a fresh hero or saint, He prints a lasting image in our minds, an abiding warm spot in our hearts, a permanent resolve in our wills. He lets us see in them what diligence can achieve in us. All of us have learned that, if we just keep on going about our business, some especially stimulating people, possibly a few of them household names, will draw near and give us a strengthening hail. And some of us have learned that on occasions of deepest need, God will provide us exactly the right person at precisely the right time. (You must be nameless here, but you know who you are.)

I should have gained at least a surface inkling of this truth even as an awestruck boy: "Hey, look quick! Over there! That's Jack Dempsey getting out of his car, right here in the middle of our town!" In that same era Bill Tilden came to display his fluid grace in exhibition tennis matches within easy bicycling distance of our home, whereupon we all attacked the game with renewed zeal. Bobby Cruikshank should have clinched the point when in qualifying for the U. S. Open Golf Championship he commandeered me, in a practice round, to give him local knowledge of the Canoe Brook course—one of the Depression jobs I had wangled was as caddy master there. "Where should I aim my drive?" he asked me as he stood on the tee of a blind hole. "Ten yards to the left of that mound at the top of the rise," I told him. His perfect tee shot disappeared from sight ten yards to the left of that mound at the top of the rise. "There?" the wee man asked with a grin. "Wow!" I said. "Exactly there," and resolved to keep on trying until, if only once, I might be able to do the same.

It is probably more important that the parish where I worked when in seminary was New York's headquarters for the monastic Order of the Holy Cross, whose members were constantly dropping in or coming to stay for a while. I could find myself server at mass to OHC's red-bearded Bishop Campbell of Liberia, home on furlough; or to Father Hughson, at that time Holy Cross's Superior; or to its Founder himself, James O. S. Huntington, who is now commemorated annually in the Church's official calendar of holy days. For half a century he has been on my private ordo, but my debt to him can never be fully repaid. People like him, and the others, leave a permanent imprint. From those heroes I learned, without any words being spoken, what priesthood really is. Just as I learned other spiritual things later on from Gert Behanna, rest her soul, and am continuing to do through Scotty Peck, who has contributed so much joy and zest to my latter years.

But as I said at the outset of this digression about people, we have all learned that if we just keep on going about our business a host of steady folk will walk miles with us along the road; others will give us a cheering hail in passing. A few of them will happen to be world-famous. Ten thousand others, equally great, will be known by name only to God, who manifestly has an infinite variety of splendid ideas as to what it is to be a real human being. Lesser lights can be true lights, too, and hence means of illumination to others. All people great and small who are seeking to become the self God has in mind for them, who are searching for what they are supposed to do and where they are supposed to do it, are of this sort. Fulfillment, satisfaction, and joy come to them because of this desire to be and do their best and spread around them to others. In the end, together we "all come . . . unto a perfect man," the only one full embodiment of that Idea, the only true Light of the world.

A few years ago my wife and I motored southward, not seeking fringe benefits but nevertheless receiving some. We passed first through Thomasville, Georgia, where former parishioners had started a new mission church—or, rather, a solid parish, sprung like Minerva full-grown, self-supporting, and flourishing from its natal day. In Tallahassee we visited another former parishioner, now retired from business and following his late vocation to holy orders as a perpetual deacon in ways that I have mentioned before.

From there we moved on to Daytona Beach, where I was to preach and officiate at a festival service on the occasion of my former parish's centenary celebration. That the physical plant and its people were flourishing vigorously and would continue to do so down the coming decades was an evident fact and a source of joy. Having thus looked happily around and forward, my wife and I looked backward, surely a proper indulgence on a centennial occasion. This had been our milieu for seven years as we struggled for our son's life. During that critical month when we had been seventeen hundred miles away, the people here had kept an endless prayer vigil on our behalf—around the clock on the day of the surgery. They had flocked to the blood bank to pour forth another kind of vitality there. They had amassed a sum of money to help defray our expenses. All this on their own initiative and without our knowledge until long after it had all been done. Fringe benefits.

After a few days in the Daytona area we drove southward to Vero Beach and Stuart, dropping in on past associates, seminary classmates, family members. Farther south we stayed the canonical three days with the Shoemakers. Don, editor emeritus of the *Miami Herald* but still turning out his powerful daily columns, was once a vestryman in Asheville and is forever a close, supremely valued, friend.

It took us a couple of weeks more to wend our leisurely way homeward from there by way of a big loop through Florida's Sarasota (more friends) and Dunedin (more kinfolk) as we headed the hard way toward southeast Georgia's Honey Creek. At the diocesan conference center there I conducted a clergy retreat, after which we lingered on a few days as guests of the bishop. The state of the Church in that area, furthered by many clerical and lay comrades of long standing, was clearly on a high level. In addition the fishing in Honey Creek was challenging, the golfing on nearby Jekyll Island and St. Simons superb. We found it irrelevant that our own golf scores were not.

This may be the proper place to interject that despite alleged improvements in technology and contrary to the claims of pitchmen, the sober fact remains that golf balls are not as good as they used to be. My whole generation, which has been long at the game, can and does testify with one unanimous voice that we are not as long off the tee as once we were. A few of us state petulantly that an industrial society able to put men on the moon should also be competent to make a golf ball lively enough to let us hit greens in regulation, yet the last time we did so was six years ago, with the wind behind us and the fairway downhill all the way.

While waiting for the technicians to get on the ball, most of us hackers have coped by adjusting our psychologies. Instead of lamenting that we *take* more strokes now than we used to, we rejoice in discerning that we *get* more. As we progressively approach the time when we get as many shots in nine holes as we used to in eighteen, we even note thankfully that this represents a great saving of time and energy, both of which, unfortunately, are in ever-shorter supply.

Like our recent visit to the old school, that survey trip taken at the ending of the day was one more fringe benefit, among so many along the way, demonstrating the whole journey's worth. The trouble with having been on one such glorious adventure, however, is that it makes you eager to keep on going. We had hardly been home long enough to wash our clothes and put things back into their accustomed places when my wife mused aloud, possibly with intent that I should overhear, "How long has it been since we went to St. Louis and Salt Lake City to see the kids?"

Of choice we lived very simply then, as now, in a place that took care of itself for weeks on end. I had not committed myself to any supply work, so our schedule put no pressure on us. Our tottery neighbor was away on a visit, hence would not feel any insecurity because of our absence. I was up-to-date in the role of Elder Statesman: the bishop had been in recently to debrief himself after the diocesan convention, and a young priest had come by after a Cursillo to discuss his vocation and a call. Our mail was answered and our bills, if not yet our dues, were fully paid. The doctors had recently overhauled us, demonstrating that Shakespeare is no longer correct in saying that the final stages of our strange eventful history must be endured sans teeth, sans eyes, sans taste. So, not many days later, we were off again. With my hearing aid in my left ear, my intraocular lens implanted in my right eye, and a mouth full of store-bought teeth, we headed off together into the setting sun. When we reached our destinations we found, just as we had suspected, that the future is in good hands.

TWENTY-SIX

Epilogue

*. . . oil and wine, bread and water,
compassion and a few kind words.*

Half a century ago, when I was a fledgling priest, I wanted the
Church to be at the forefront of the human journey. I wanted her to
be an intrepid Amazon, sword in one hand and searchlight in the
other, striding purposefully forward against all odds, lighting the
path and clearing the way so that the human race could safely
follow. Unfortunately, the Church I observed seemed more like an
ambulance following in the wake of progress, making clucking
noises as it picked up those fallen by the wayside and applied Band-
Aids to their wounds.

I even wondered at the efficacy of those Band-Aids. All around
me and within me I found eternal wonderings and bone weariness;
sickness, pain, sin, and evil; guilt, fear, dashed hope and despair;
tragedy, transitoriness, death, and ultimate silence. What antidotes
did the Church have against all that? What was her response to

elemental mystery and universal misery? Nothing more than the pharmacopeia of the Good Samaritan: oil and wine, bread and water, compassion and a few kind words. What good were those things in dire circumstances, in extreme situations when thieves fall upon a traveler to beat him, strip him, rob him, and leave him in a ditch half-dead?

So half a century ago I would think: "Comes the Revolution, we clergy will be the first to go. We nonproducers will be unmasked as dilettantes mouthing empty words. We will be classified as inconsequential and irrelevant; entirely unnecessary to human welfare and frequently harmful to it. So, comes the Revolution, we might be put to some practical use in the salt mines. More probably we will simply be lined up against a wall and shot."

Meanwhile I did keep on baptizing and anointing, saying prayers, reading the Bible, preaching and absolving, marrying and burying, offering Eucharist and giving Holy Communion—once again, that was all the armory I had. In so doing I discovered that those simple acts conveyed reality. Somewhat to my astonishment they had observable power in human life. To my startled joy they manifestly overmastered evil. All around me, because of them the blind saw, the lame walked, lepers were cleansed, the deaf heard, the dead were raised. And one fine day I even realized that the Church as ambulance is in itself the Church as light shining in darkness. In this new and certain knowledge I reread the Prologue to St. John's Gospel, lifted up my head, and spoke boldly as I ought to speak.

Notably I have also found reality in the Church's ceremonies, power in her actions, truth in her words, and substance behind the shadow, during the past forty days, because six weeks ago my wife of fifty-six years died suddenly and unexpectedly, at the end of an enjoyed and purposeful day. Since then I have not so much been an officiant at the Church's sacraments, a celebrant of her rites and ceremonies, a minister of friendship, counsel, and loving care, as a grateful recipient of these heavenly things. Others, clergy and laity by the score, have sprung up out of the ground to minister them to me. In this bedrock experience I find, most personally, that the Good Samaritan's oil and wine continue to be restorative; indeed, to be the only restoratives there are. They are "the gifts of God for the people of God." Although brought by intermediaries, they come directly from The Source of Power, and they convey it, or Him. They enable us to stand on our feet, to get back on the path, and to resume our journey straight ahead, sword in one hand and search-light in the other.